INNER SEX
IN 30 DAYS

INNER SEX
IN 30 DAYS

THE EROTIC FULFILLMENT PROGRAM

KEITH HARARY, PH.D., AND PAMELA WEINTRAUB

ST. MARTIN'S PRESS NEW YORK

Library of Congress Cataloging-in-Publication Data

Harary, Keith.
　　Inner sex in 30 days : the erotic fulfillment program / Keith
Harary and Pamela Weintraub.
　　　　p.　cm.
　　ISBN 0-312-05103-4
　　1. Sex instruction.　2. Sex customs.　I. Weintraub, Pamela.
II. Title.　III. Title: Inner sex in thirty days.
HQ31.H343　1990
613.9'6—dc20　　　　　　　　　　　　　　　　　　　　90-36876
　　　　　　　　　　　　　　　　　　　　　　　　　　　　CIP

First Edition: September 1990

10 9 8 7 6 5 4 3 2 1

For our partners,
Darlene Moore and Mark Teich

CONTENTS

INTRODUCTION

*H*ave you ever wished your lover could instinctively respond to your innermost sexual fantasies, almost as if she could read your mind? Would you like your sex partner to react naturally to your deepest urges, as if his secret cravings were the erotic counterpoint to your own? Have you ever wished you could satisfy your lover's most intimate sexual needs before he or she even realized they had entertained such desires at all? Finally, would you like your sex life to move beyond mere physical performance to heightened levels of mutual gratification and emotional connectedness, almost as if your lovemaking took place on a transcendent, mystical plane?

If these are your goals, then *Inner Sex in 30 Days: The Erotic Fulfillment Program* can be your guide. By practicing the mental imaging and sensitivity exercises presented in this practical, step-by-step, and clinically based book, you can experience expanded levels of sexual arousal and fulfillment.

For instance, in one exercise you will sit on the floor facing your lover in a candle-lit room, observing each other's naked bodies in the soft, flickering light. Though the exercise will not include actual physical contact, you will experience intense sexual arousal and may even come to understand your partner far more intimately than you have in the past. In another exercise, you will gently kiss, scratch, and bite your lover in special places, causing his or her entire body to reverberate with the sort of passion usually reserved for full-blown sexual intercourse and orgasm.

In yet another exercise, you will imagine yourself immersed in some ancient or future society, one that regularly practices sexual rites you have rehearsed only in your mind. You will see your secret world down to the last detail, from the leather thongs, lush fur togas, and amethyst studs worn by the inhabitants to the vast crystal chambers where they live and sleep. Then you will imagine the sex—soft and spontaneous, under a torrent of sunlight, for instance, or impassioned, even rough, atop the wet clay mounds that serve as beds. Later that evening you will share your scenario with your partner, who has imagined a secret society of his or her own. As the night goes on, you and your lover will reenact the scenarios, wrapping yourselves in an airtight envelope where the two secret societies have mystically merged.

Through such exercises, the Erotic Fulfillment Program will teach you to increase your sensual awareness, bringing repressed sexual urges and hidden fantasies to light. It will also help you and your lover tune into each other's innermost sexual desires and private erotic dreams. As you follow the 30-day program, in fact, you will not only improve your sex life and move closer to fulfilling your most personal sexual fantasies, but will also add depth and inspiration to the broader aspects of your ongoing love relationships.

Most books about human sexuality place a heavy emphasis on the physical techniques of lovemaking or apparent sexual dysfunction. These "manuals" often describe sex in terms reminiscent of athletic competition. While such books may be useful for learning about certain basic sexual techniques, they often overemphasize the *goals* of sexual gamesmanship while ignoring the more profound and private, often *transcendent*, feelings associated with passionate sexual love. Thus, instead of bringing lovers closer together and creating a mutual emotional refuge from the demands of everyday life, current sex books frequently carry the performance pressures and anxieties of the working world into the bedroom; they encourage, rather than alleviate, underlying sexual frustration and stress. What's more, they don't even begin to tap sex as a tool for exploring one's self, one's relationship, one's environment, and the deeper mysteries of the universe.

The Erotic Fulfillment Program, however, rejects the high-pressure approach to sexual performance. Instead, our 30-day program taps a series of visualization and guided imagery techniques to transport you into the expanded realm of mutual sexual communication, trust, and *inner* exploration. Combining the findings of current clinical studies in human sexuality with deep relaxation, sensory awareness, and interpersonal sensitivity techniques, the Inner Sex exercises will help you to intensify your sexual awareness and responsiveness; they will also help you to use eroticism as a pathway to mutual understanding, fulfillment, and even higher consciousness. Indeed, sex experienced through the Erotic Fulfillment Program should not only prove deeply pleasant and intense on a primal level, it may also induce a sense of timelessness, a sense of inner connection to the universe, insights into the nature of reality, and even a sense of reverie or bliss.

The Inner Sex exercises take you on this spiraling erotic journey a step at a time, starting with the basic sensitivity training of Week One. During this first week, you will learn to become more consciously aware of your innermost subconscious sexual thoughts and feelings. You will also tune in to your five senses, developing an increasingly erotic relationship with your body and your surrounding environment. And you will learn to induce the altered state of alert relaxation, in which your body enters a state of deep relaxation while your mind remains acutely alert. In this heightened mental state, you will use guided imagery exercises to envision your deepest sexual fantasies and tap the core of your inner sexual self.

In Week Two, you will explore your heightened sensuality in a series of erotic realization exercises to be practiced with a partner. You will start with simple techniques such as talking to and working out with your partner. You will then move on to exercises in tactile and auditory stimulation. And, finally, you will learn to deepen the erotic bond between you and your lover by inducing a shared sexual dream.

In Week Three of the Erotic Fulfillment Program, you will build upon the knowledge and heightened sensitivities developed during the first two weeks. The goal for Week Three: to enhance sexual intuition so that lovemaking is far more spontaneous and instinctive than it was before. In one exercise, for example, you will engage in the art of pantomime, acting out your most exotic romantic and sexual fantasies for a lover, who will then help you reenact the fantasy in bed. And, through a series of ''transpersonal focusing'' techniques, you and your lover will envision the world through each other's eyes. Week Three encompasses the core techniques for true Inner Sex, and should help you become a lover with potent intuitive skills.

During Week Four you will explore the connection between your heightened erotic awareness and the realm of higher consciousness, including mystical experiences, enhanced intuition, and intensified states of sexual fulfillment. In one Week Four exercise, for example, you will use your enhanced erotic sensitivity to experience a deeper sense of connection to the Earth. In another, you will immerse yourself in the powerful altered state induced through orgasm, experiencing transcendent feelings of timelessness and a sense of connection to the cosmos at large.

As you explore and experience the Erotic Fulfillment Program, there are a few things we would like you to keep in mind. First of all, many couples will find it difficult to carry out this program in its entirety in exactly 30 days. Do not feel that the 30-day time frame is an absolute. Instead, take your time with the Inner Sex techniques and don't pressure yourself or your sexual partner. Practice each day's activities only when you and your lover are both open to sharing profound emotional and sexual experiences with each other and when you both have time to integrate the results. If a particular exercise turns you or your partner off, just skip it and move on to the next technique instead.

You may find, moreover, that different exercises affect you and your partner in different ways. Allow your partner room to respond differently than you. Do not force things, and continue to talk to your partner about how he or she feels about the exercises throughout. Remember, the Erotic Fulfillment Program is meant to be savored, shared, and explored at a pace, and in a fashion, that feels good for all involved.

We also want to point out that the Inner Sex exercises are meant to help you and your partner realize your *individual* erotic potential, as well as the erotic potential you share as a couple. In other words, there are no absolutes. We do not suggest that you have a specific number of orgasms each hour, or that you try three innovative sexual positions a day. Rather, these exercises set the stage so that you can *explore* your inner eroticism, establishing adventures, patterns, and rituals that you deem appropriate for yourselves.

For the most part, the Inner Sex exercises are geared to couples. After all, as a recent survey commissioned by the editors of *Psy-*

chology Today showed, more and more people are becoming monogamous, having sex in couples, and, in general, giving up those one-night stands. The sexually promiscuous Sixties and Seventies have long since been replaced by the sexually committed Nineties. Yet the sexual revolution isn't over, it's just matured in the past twenty-five years. If you want to grow along with it—to experience erotic actualization through greater sensual sensitivity and deeper feelings of connectedness to the universe, your lover, and yourself— the Erotic Fulfillment Program can help light the way.

While advocating long-term relationships where possible, the Erotic Fulfillment Program is not designed exclusively for those in couple relationships. Our exercises are also powerful tools for those who do not have a regular sex partner. Simply practicing many of the exercises should help you respond on a more instinctive level even to part-time or first-time lovers. (In these instances, please remember to practice safe sex!) And for those who have chosen or are bearing with celibacy for the moment, the exercises can, with a little imagination, be practiced completely alone. If you are in this group, Inner Sex can enrich your fantasy life and expand your erotic horizons as well.

We want to emphasize that it would be most unusual for anyone to report problems as a result of the Erotic Fulfillment Program, especially since the program does not attempt to replace psychotherapy, sex therapy, or couples counseling in any way. However, if you have a history of emotional or psychiatric problems, or if you feel at all uncomfortable about any of the exercises, we suggest you check with a therapist or psychiatrist before proceeding. In such a case, you might wish to carry out the Erotic Fulfillment Program only under his or her continued clinical guidance. Of course, these exercises should be practiced only by consenting adults.

No matter who you are, the Inner Sex exercises have been designed for your enjoyment. As you work your way through the program, your erotic experience should become increasingly expansive, powerful, and deep. So why not get started, beginning with a celebration of your own body in Week One. It's a "come as you are" party. We'll bring the hats.

WEEK ONE

THE SENSUAL SELF

WEEK ONE

•

THE SENSUAL
SELF

All of life is a sensual experience. During Week One of the Erotic Fulfillment Program, your goal will be to tune in to the sensuous nature of your everyday life. Once you do so, you should be capable of what we call "inner sex," in which your sexuality emerges from the deepest, most essential part of yourself.

To experience true inner sex—to commune with your lover on the most intimate of levels—you must first learn to get more closely in touch with your own body, including all your senses. After all, to fully connect with your lover on a sensual plane, you must first be thoroughly connected to your own sexual potential, feelings, and desires. You must know who you are, what you want, and what you like to do. Not only will this self-knowledge enable you to get more enjoyment out of sex, it will help you comprehend on the deepest of levels how to heighten your partner's sexual enjoyment as well.

Toward that end, you will begin Week One simply by exploring the sensory pleasures of an orange—from its brilliant color to its sweet/pungent taste to the dimpled feel of its skin. You will then set out to create an *erotic refuge*—a private environment in which you can freely explore your inner sexuality alone and with a partner while leaving the rest of the world outside. Secure in your erotic refuge, you can express your inner erotic identity by drawing mandalas and reach ever greater levels of sexual arousal through powerful "self-pleasuring" techniques.

During Week One, you will also learn to induce the altered state of consciousness known as alert relaxation, in which the body be-comes increasingly relaxed while the mind remains alert. Athletes often enter this altered state of consciousness to mentally rehearse their maneuvers. Cancer patients also draw upon this state to rally their immune systems to fight the intrusive disease that threatens their lives. In the Erotic Fulfillment Program you tap this same powerful mental state to become more sensitive to your own body, your deepest fantasies, and your inner sexual self.

The techniques of Week One, of course, should be carried out more or less on your own. While practicing the Week One exercises, remember to keep your body healthy and clean. Keep up with a physical fitness program, be it an aerobics class, running, or simply brisk walks a few times a week. Also maintain a healthy diet low in fat and high in complex carbohydrates. Eat plenty of sweet, sensual fruits. By treating your body with care and respect and practicing the Week One exercises presented here, you will be well prepared for the three weeks of heightened inner eroticism to come.

DAY 1

FORBIDDEN FRUIT

In one of our all-time favorite short features, cre-ated by filmmaker Karen Johnson, the camera focuses so closely on the navel of an orange that we initially believe we are viewing the sexual organs of a beautiful woman. As the camera pans around the peel, the orange gradually spreads open before us, and we come to recognize that we are observing a piece of fruit. Despite the reali-zation, there is still something compellingly sensuous about the image that fills the screen.

To become more attuned to your personal sexual potential, you must first get more in touch with *all* of your senses. We suggest you start by examining a piece of fruit.

Pick up an orange and look at it closely. Notice its rich, orange color, including any subtle variations in particular spots. Notice its weight and the cool, curved feeling of its skin touching yours. Then slowly roll it around in your hands and feel its shape gently yielding to your fingers as you lightly squeeze it.

Now slowly begin peeling the orange. As you do so, notice the feeling of your fingertips piercing the skin and carefully pulling it away from the inner fruit. Listen to the sound of the skin being pulled apart, and notice the sharp aroma of orange oil drifting into the atmosphere as the peel itself is broken. Notice the aroma growing stronger as you hold the orange closer to your face.

Now pull apart the inner sections so that the entire fruit is spread open in your hands like a soft, orange crystal. Feel the wetness of the orange, notice the softer aroma of its inner juices and the way the surrounding light reflects on its crystalline surfaces.

Finally, completely pull apart the orange and put one entire section in your mouth. Feel its soft wetness on your lips and tongue, then gently pierce it with your teeth and feel the fresh orange juice squirting into your mouth. Feel the texture of the innermost part of the orange on the inside of your mouth. Chew the orange until you have extracted the sweet, pungent *orangeness* that is the essence of this fruit. Then swallow and feel the orange moving down your throat and into your body. As you consume the rest of the orange, continue paying full attention to all of your senses in the same fashion.

Sensual Suggestion—You may repeat this exercise as often as you like throughout the four weeks of the Erotic Fulfillment Program and, of course, beyond. In the future, moreover, you may wish to use a variety of other citrus fruits, including tangerines, grapefruits, lemons, limes, and tangelos. We also recommend expanding this exercise to include a variety of sensuous berries—raspberries, blackberries, strawberries, blueberries, and cranberries—and such stimulating fruits as kiwis, pineapples, and mangoes. (Try cutting a kiwi or a mango in half and sucking out the insides with your lips and tongue.) Compare the many different types of sensory experiences that you have with each of these fruits, paying attention not only to their very different tastes, but also to the different ways they smell, sound, and feel in your hands and mouth.

DAY 2

EROTIC REFUGE

Begin today's exercise by sitting in the middle of your bedroom and calmly looking around. Is your bedroom a sensual environment especially conducive to the expression of your inner sexuality? Do the colors and textures work to enhance your sexuality, or to repress it? Is your bedroom a soft, inviting refuge from the world at large? Or does the outside world intrude itself into this private realm in subtle or not-so-subtle ways?

For instance, does your bedroom window look out upon a magnificent ocean vista, or across a narrow, garbage can–filled alley directly into the kitchen window of the apartment next door? Are books or papers from work piled on a desk or table, or lying on the floor around your bed? Have you left your clothes and shoes in a heap by the door? Is the bed a comfortable place where you can luxuriate in the full-blown throes of spontaneous sexual passion, a convertible sofa bed that must be pulled out before you can go to sleep, or a worn-out, lumpy mattress you found on the sidewalk five years ago, then dragged home and threw on the floor? Does a television set occupy such a central position in the room that you can't avoid looking directly at it while lying in bed on your back? What sort of pictures, if any, are hanging on your walls?

Once you have taken a mental inventory of your bedroom environment, you should move to transform it into an *erotic refuge*. Your erotic refuge should be a room in which you can emotionally leave the outside world *outside*. It should, most of all, be a completely safe and private realm in which you may tune in to and explore your sexuality in a totally uninhibited way.

Turning your bedroom into an erotic zone may take several days and require a small investment. But the effort will be worth it, paying dividends by enhancing your overall emotional state and your level of sexual awareness. We suggest that you begin transforming your bedroom environment today. If appropriate, you may share the experience with your partner as a way of reaffirming your commitment to your emotional and sexual relationship.

Begin by clearing the room of any objects that make it seem cluttered or distract you from feeling fully focused on your sexual

partner. Do not enter this particular room unless you have first re-
moved your shoes. Also make sure the room is strictly a bedroom
—clear it of any objects that make the room seem partly living room,
say, or partly bathroom or office or closet.

> **Sensual Suggestion**—To avoid the feel of a closet, arrange the room
> so you won't be tempted to just toss your clothes on the floor. Re-
> organize the dresser drawers or closet especially for this purpose, or
> set up a corner chair where you can neatly hang your clothes after
> taking them off.

> **Sensual Suggestion**—If your quarters are cramped, and you must
> use your bedroom for more than one purpose—for instance, if you must
> equip it with a desk and computer—try to use screens, colorful cloth
> 'hangings, or curtains to divide the distracting area off. Even if you
> live in a studio apartment, you can still turn a corner of it into an
> enticing erotic zone that exists apart from the rest of the apartment
> and the world around it.

Remove from your erotic refuge any object, picture, or piece of
furniture that reminds you of any former lovers. (If this is impossible,
just change the room as much as possible and rearrange the furniture
for a fresh start.) Clean the room thoroughly so that you feel completely comfortable touching any surface—including the floor—with
your totally naked body. If the room is desperately in need of paint,
go ahead and paint it. Choose soothing, sexually stimulating colors
such as mauve, pale scarlet, or champagne.

Also pay particular attention to art or decorations adorning your
wall. Art should reflect your innermost erotic desires and tastes,
whatever they may be. However, wall decorations often work best
on your unconscious mind when they are subtle. A still life of hot
pink peaches or uncut fruit may be more sexually suggestive than a
current pinup, for instance. A picture of roving lions or athletes
stretching to cross the finish line may—or, depending upon your
taste, may not—be more titillating than a pornographic photo. You
may also feel turned on by impressionistic drawings, photographs
or paintings of dancers, or by pictures of you and your lover together
at various moments in your lives.

If the room is not carpeted, place a comfortable throw rug, big
enough for you and your lover to stretch out upon, on the floor. Put

some fresh plants or flowers in the room, along with other natural objects such as seashells, feathers, colorful rocks, or fossils. An aquarium with exotic and colorful tropical fish and internal lights is particularly sensual. So are red or pink light bulbs, which may be purchased in a variety store and placed in any lamp.

> **Sensual Suggestion**—Red light may endow you and your lover with an ethereal, almost otherworldly appearance. Many people find that the red glow intensifies erotic communication and sexual arousal.

Make sure that your erotic refuge is absolutely private. If your window looks out on a beautiful setting, make sure that no one within that setting may peer in. If your view is less than comforting or serene, cover your window with an attractive shade, blind, or curtain. Soft fabrics are particularly sensual. If the room feels small and confining, expand its optical dimensions with mirrors or broad areas of contrasting color.

> **Sensual Suggestion**—No matter what the size of your room, we suggest you set up at least one attractive full-length mirror. This will be essential in many of the exercises that follow. We do not believe it is necessary, however, to go so far as to mirror the ceiling above your bed.

Pay special attention to the condition and position of your bed. Cover the bed in clean sheets and a comforter or blanket, using soft textures that feel especially comfortable next to your bare skin. Toss a variety of different-sized pillows on the bed, not just the more traditional pillows that most of us are accustomed to using when we go to sleep. If at all possible, your bed should occupy the central position in the room. It should be absolutely clean and thoroughly comfortable.

If you feel you cannot survive without a television in your bedroom, leave it unplugged and place it in the corner. In the same fashion, if there is a telephone in your bedroom, switch it off or unplug it whenever you are about to use the room as an erotic refuge and do not wish to be disturbed. (If need be, hook up an answering machine to the phone line in an adjacent room so that you won't be distracted by concerns over missing important calls.)

Arrange a source of music for your erotic refuge. Whether you choose a turntable, CD, or tape player, you should ideally be able to adjust the volume and change the musical selections without having to leave the room for another part of your home. If this is impossible, then there should be speakers leading into the room from your musical source, which should be able to play a continuous series of musical selections for at least an hour to an hour and a half. We suggest that you avoid using a radio to provide the musical background for your erotic refuge. Radio announcers are notorious for destroying the mood of a piece of music by talking over the beginning and end of a song and for broadcasting commercials between selections. The radio also offers you little personal choice over the specific musical selections you'll be hearing.

Complete your erotic refuge with a fantasy wardrobe to be worn whenever you and your partner are at home alone together. Contemporary clothing is often tight and overtailored, dividing the body into different segments with such things as tight belts and ties. Zippers and buttons can also hinder eroticism, as can the feeling of synthetic fabrics against your skin. As a more erotic change of pace, try to get into the habit of changing into loose, flowing clothes when you return home at the end of the day. Even if this isn't always practical, you should still change into such clothes whenever you and your partner are about to share a sexual encounter in your erotic refuge. We suggest wearing such items as silk and satin kimonos, robes, or pajamas. These sensual garments, which should allow you to experience the natural and uninhibited sexuality of your body, are preferable to the overstated fashions you generally find in erotic-wear boutiques.

Finally, we suggest that you consider the bathroom closest to your bedroom. In the course of the Erotic Fulfillment Program, you will be sharing romantic and sexually stimulating baths and showers with your partner. Beyond this, the state of your bathroom environment is an intimate expression of how you feel about your body. It is the room in which you clean your body in preparation for a sexual encounter, and it is often the room in which you will find yourself —for one reason or another—either during a sexual experience or shortly after a sexual encounter is completed. It should therefore be kept scrupulously clean and inviting, using the same sorts of general techniques you used in preparing your erotic bedroom environment.

Place a clean and cozy rug on the bathroom floor, and make sure there are plenty of clean, large, thick, and absorbent cotton towels available at all times. It is often not the most exotic sex aids that make the difference in our enjoyment of a given sexual encounter, but, rather, the simple niceties of life.

In addition, the bathroom should not be the place where you store your beloved collection of exotic mushrooms or your ten-year collection of *Popular Mechanics* magazines. Rather, it should be a well-kept erotic environment that openly expresses your inner sensitivity to your own and your partner's sexuality.

DAY 3

INSIDE MOVES

As children, most of us have enormous intuitive and imaginative resources. However, we often lose touch with these qualities as adults. Writers, musicians, and artists are sometimes exceptions, tapping these inner resources to create their most powerful works. Their creations are sometimes said to "pop into" their minds from "someplace else"—as if the words or music on a page have been transcribed from some "inner dictation," or as if an "inner artist" has guided the application of paint to canvas.

Of course, the inner writer, artist, or musician is not a manifestation of some outside force but, rather, an active expression of that individual's innermost imagination. Often, this inner voice gives rise to more true passion and insight than our conscious, analytic selves. To help you tap your own inner voice, we present an elaborate guided imagery technique, in which you will follow instructions prerecorded on tape. While today's exercise, practiced in a warm, sensual bath, does not require that you focus on specific, sexual images, it should awaken your inner muse. The result should be enhanced performance in a variety of creative activities, including your ability to experience a more intuitive form of sex.

Sensual Suggestion—Because the exercise for Day 3 is rather complex, we suggest that you read all the instructions twice before proceeding.

To get in touch with your unconscious self on Day 3, you must first enter the altered state of *alert relaxation*, in which the mind remains alert while the body becomes extremely relaxed. Athletes often enter this altered state of consciousness to mentally rehearse their maneuvers. The combination of relaxation and alertness allows them to establish a deep communion with their bodies; finely tuned mental control of muscle movements is often the result. In the same way, alert relaxation will help you mentally explore—and ultimately intensify—your deepest, most sensual feelings. A new appreciation of your emotional, sexual self should emerge.

After you have entered the state of alert relaxation, you will mentally drift for three minutes. Then the guided-imagery part of the exercise (adapted in part from techniques described in *Sexual Secrets* by Nik Douglas and Penny Slinger) can begin.

To prepare, first have a special lover or friend record the instructions below on a cassette recorder. You should listen to the tape while enjoying a hot bath.

> **Sensual Suggestion**—If, like many Erotic Fulfillment Program partici-
> pants, you are moving through all the exercises with a single partner,
> you may make tapes for each other. If you prefer to practice this
> exercise completely on your own, you may record the instructions
> yourself.

The person reading the instructions should speak slowly and pause for the amount of time indicated. When the word PAUSE appears alone, simply pause for a second or two. The words to be recorded follow.

> Take a deep breath, let it out slowly, stretch your muscles, and relax.
> Now imagine that warm currents of mental energy are very slowly
> moving up through the soles of your feet toward your ankles.

●

> Feel the muscles in your feet gradually warming and relaxing as you
> imagine the currents passing through them. [PAUSE] Imagine that the
> currents continue moving up through your calves, [PAUSE] into your
> thighs, [PAUSE] through your hips [PAUSE] and buttocks, [PAUSE] and
> into your lower back and abdomen. [PAUSE] Proceed very slowly,
> giving yourself time for each group of muscles to begin fully relaxing

before allowing the imaginary currents to move on to the next area of your body. [PAUSE] Feel the muscles in your legs becoming heavy, warm, and relaxed, and sinking down into the tub beneath you. [PAUSE]

●

When you feel your legs becoming deeply relaxed, imagine the currents moving in a clockwise motion around your abdomen, [PAUSE] up along your spine, [PAUSE] and through the front of your torso into your chest [PAUSE] and shoulders. Feel the muscles in your stomach and lower back releasing any tightness or tension as the current passes through them. [PAUSE] Allow a feeling of general well-being to begin flowing through your body along with the imaginary currents as you continue to relax. [PAUSE]

●

When the lower half of your body feels relaxed, [PAUSE] imagine the currents flowing upward through your ribs and shoulders [PAUSE]— warming and relaxing the upper part of your body [PAUSE] and leaving your back and chest feeling completely warm and free of any stress or tension. [PAUSE] Imagine the currents turning around to move downward through your arms and toward your fingertips; [PAUSE] imagine the current swirling around through your fingers and hands and then moving upward once more, [PAUSE] back through your arms and neck [PAUSE] toward the top of your head. [PAUSE]

●

Now feel the muscles in your neck and face gradually becoming warm and relaxed as the imaginary currents pass through them. [PAUSE] Then imagine the currents flowing out through the top of your head, [PAUSE] leaving your entire body feeling comfortably warm, [PAUSE] heavy, [PAUSE] and relaxed, [PAUSE] and sinking down into the tub beneath you. [PAUSE] Now allow yourself to drift. Feel your body becoming increasingly relaxed, and see the image of a completely blank screen in your mind. Continue to focus on this image for the next three minutes. If you must focus on something besides a blank screen, envision an endless white field of snow. [PAUSE FOR THREE MINUTES]

●

Now close your eyes and focus on images of expansion and contraction. Many things in nature expand and then contract, including stars, galaxies, and perhaps even the universe itself. Spend a few seconds visualizing one of these cosmic systems expanding and contracting, expanding and contracting again, and again. [PAUSE]

●

Our human bodies also expand and contract. In fact, in all sexuality, expansion and contraction play pivotal roles. Allow your thoughts to drift into images of sexual expansion and contraction. See your chest and your partner's chest expanding and contracting with excitement. See your heart and your partner's heart expanding and contracting with the effort of making love. See your sex organs and your partner's sex organs expanding and contracting together. Hold this image in your mind for several seconds. [PAUSE FOR FIVE SECONDS]

●

Now imagine your body expanding into the warm water surrounding you. [PAUSE] Then picture your body contracting back into itself. See it expanding and contracting in the warm water, s-l-o-w-l-y expanding and contracting, again and again. [PAUSE FOR ONE MINUTE]

●

See yourself returning to your normal size and once more focus on the notion of emptiness. Consider how much of the universe consists of emptiness. Envision the emptiness of outer space, the open sky, the surface of the ocean, and the submicroscopic spaces within individual molecules and atoms. Continue focusing on these images of emptiness until your mind seems all but devoid of any extraneous thoughts. To hold this feeling of emptiness, continue to picture a totally blank screen or a white, endless field of snow. [PAUSE FOR ONE MINUTE]

●

Now focus on the emptiness within your body. See the spaces between your internal organs, and the vast spaces between the individual atoms that comprise your physical form. Breathe slowly, deeply, into your diaphragm, and focus on the air entering and leaving your body. Envision your body as a transparent container of emptiness—as empty as the vacuum of outer space—floating in the comfort of the warm, soothing bathwater surrounding you. Inhale, and feel the surface of the container expand. Exhale, and feel the surface of the container contract. Focus on your breath flowing in and out. Feel the soft envelope of your body expanding and contracting as you breathe.

●

Continue to breathe in and out, in and out. Recall your earlier images of the natural universe expanding and contracting. Now imagine your body—and your entire being down to your individual atoms—expanding and contracting in harmony with nature. Feel your individual existence flowing in continuous harmony with every other living and nonliving aspect of nature. Feel your heart expanding and contracting within your body and imagine it is the central force driving the expansion and contraction of the entire universe within and around you. [PAUSE]

●

Finally, imagine that your body provides an inner window to all events in the natural world. Picture a portal in the center of your stomach. Look through it and see the surf of your blood pounding the rocky coastline of your arteries and veins. Feel the rhythms of your body moving in harmony with these eternal waves, and imagine that you are drawing the power of the ocean into your innermost being.

●

Look through the portal again and see a great black stallion climbing the cliffs of your muscles and bones. Imagine your own heart beating in rhythm with the heart of this inner beast. Imagine that you are merging with the animal, drawing some of its wild energy into your innermost being and giving it some of your human energy in return. [PAUSE]

●

Now it is time for you to return to complete waking consciousness. Wiggle your fingers and toes, open your eyes and look around you, and enjoy the rest of your bath.

Sensual Suggestion—Label this tape for future use and reference. Break off the tabs on the back of the cassette so that you do not accidentally record over it.

You may begin the actual exercise anytime after the instructions have been recorded. We suggest, however, that you choose a time when you won't be disturbed. Also make sure you practice the exercise while alert and unlikely to fall asleep entering the state of deep relaxation. First, go to the bathroom and run water for a warm (not hot), soothing bath. If possible, turn the bathroom lights down low. (If it is nighttime, you might light a candle or simply let light filter in from an adjacent room.) Remember to turn on the tape recorder and put it someplace where it won't fall into the water or get wet in any way. Then climb into the bathtub and enjoy!

Sensual Suggestion—It is extremely unlikely that you will fall asleep while in the state of alert relaxation. Just in case you do, however, please have a close friend or lover nearby during this exercise. This individual does not have to sit by you, but should simply peek in every ten minutes or so to make sure you are awake.

Sensual Suggestion—If you feel that burning some incense will enhance your mood during this exercise, then please feel free to do so.

Sensual Suggestion—If you have time, you might want to practice a shortened version of this exercise every day or so throughout the duration of the Erotic Fulfillment Program. To practice the shortened version of Inside Moves, you need not use your recorder and cassette tape. Instead, enter the state of alert relaxation on your own by breathing slowly and deeply and imagining warm currents of energy gradually moving up through the soles of your feet and throughout every muscle in your body. Take as much time as you feel you need to comfortably achieve a state of alert relaxation. Then, in your mind's eye, play back natural and biological images of expansion and contraction. Finally, look through your body's portal to glimpse the world within. You may practice the shortened version of Inside Moves in or out of the bath.

DAY 4

SEXUAL CENTER

Today you will search for your inner sexual self. Before you do so, you must ask a friend or lover to record a second tape for you. This tape, like the one you had made yesterday, will consist of an induction for alert relaxation. However, instead of guided imagery suggestions for expansion, contraction, and communion, you will follow the alert relaxation part of the tape with 30 minutes of music.

The music you select for this tape should not contain lyrics. Instead, we suggest that you find 30 minutes of baroque music, which moves to the tempo of 60 to 70 beats per minute, much like the resting human heart. This music, researchers say, seems to induce a sense of calm and can help you to stay alert but relaxed. Appropriate baroque composers include Vivaldi, Schubert, Handel, and Haydn. If you simply do not like baroque music, you may choose another style. However, we suggest that you stay away from experimental jazz, which you might find jarring, and New Age compositions, which might be so soporific that they lull you to sleep.

If possible, recruit the same friend or lover who recorded the Inside Moves tape for you and have him or her read the instructions below:

Take a deep breath, let it out slowly, stretch your muscles, and relax. Now imagine that warm currents of mental energy are very slowly moving up through the soles of your feet toward your ankles.

●

Feel the muscles in your feet gradually warming and relaxing as you imagine the currents passing through them. [PAUSE] Imagine that the currents continue moving up through your calves, [PAUSE] into your thighs, [PAUSE] through your hips [PAUSE] and buttocks, [PAUSE] and into your lower back and abdomen. [PAUSE] Proceed very slowly, giving yourself time for each group of muscles to begin fully relaxing before allowing the imaginary currents to move on to the next area of your body. [PAUSE] Feel the muscles in your legs becoming heavy, warm, and relaxed and sinking down into the chair beneath you. [PAUSE]

●

When you feel your legs becoming deeply relaxed, imagine the currents moving in a clockwise motion around your abdomen, [PAUSE] up along your spine, [PAUSE] and through the front of your torso into your chest [PAUSE] and shoulders. Feel the muscles in your stomach and lower back releasing any tightness or tension as the current passes through them. [PAUSE] Allow a feeling of general well-being to begin flowing through your body along with the imaginary currents as you continue to relax. [PAUSE]

●

When the lower half of your body feels relaxed, [PAUSE] imagine the currents flowing upward through your ribs and shoulders [PAUSE]—warming and relaxing the upper part of your body [PAUSE] and leaving your back and chest feeling completely warm and free of any stress or tension. [PAUSE] Imagine the currents turning around to move downward through your arms and toward your fingertips; [PAUSE] imagine the current swirling around through your fingers and hands and then moving upward once more, [PAUSE] back through your arms and neck [PAUSE] toward the top of your head. [PAUSE]

●

Now feel the muscles in your neck and face gradually becoming warm and relaxed as the imaginary currents pass through them. [PAUSE] Then imagine the currents flowing out through the top of your head, [PAUSE] leaving your entire body feeling comfortably warm, [PAUSE] heavy, [PAUSE] and relaxed, [PAUSE] and sinking down into the chair beneath you. [PAUSE] Now allow yourself to drift. Feel your body becoming increasingly relaxed, and empty your mind of thought. Focus on thoughts of a totally blank screen or an endless field of snow for the next three minutes.

Now add 30 minutes of music to the tape. After you have completed your tape, label it "relaxation and music tape" and break off the tabs so you will not record over it.

When you have a 45-minute stretch of time, retire to your erotic refuge and change into the loose, flowing clothing you have gathered this week. Then turn on your tape recorder and play your tape.

As soon as the music starts playing, we would like you to focus on the feelings coursing through your body. Still in the state of alert relaxation, tune in to your innermost consciousness. What is the relationship between the innermost recesses of your mind and your physical, sensual body? Is there an aspect of your conscious awareness that you experience as sexual, in and of itself, apart from your body? Conversely, are there aspects of your physical sexuality that seem somehow detached from your deepest sense of self? Imagine these different aspects of your identity merging so that your body feels like a natural extension of your innermost consciousness and your native, sexual self.

Continue to maintain this alert/relaxed focus for at least 20 or 30 minutes. Finally, gradually bring yourself back to full waking consciousness by moving your fingers and wiggling your toes, then slowly moving the rest of your body and getting up.

Get dressed and, as you do so, continue focusing upon the sensuous, sexual feelings in your body. Notice the way you move, and feel the swish of your clothing as it flows around you.

Complete this exercise by standing in front of your full-length mirror. As you gaze at your reflection, see your inner sexuality radiating out. Ask yourself if your patterns of dress and movement are an adequate expression of this part of yourself. If not, consider adjusting your wardrobe or appearance. We do not advise, however, that you overstate the sexual aspect of your personal existence through your demeanor or dress.

> ***Sensual Suggestion***—You may find it helpful to use the sexual self-relaxation and music tape whenever you want to focus on your sexuality, or whenever you simply wish to relax. We will ask you to take this tape out and use it to aid the visualization process from time to time throughout the Erotic Fulfillment Program.

DAY 5

ONE ON ONE

Have you ever wondered what your partner feels like as he or she experiences your body in a sexual way? To achieve this perspective, examine your naked body in front of a full-length mirror. We suggest that you carry out this exercise during the afternoon, or at some other time of the day when you are generally unaccustomed to seeing yourself completely naked and are especially likely to be alert. For reasons that should be entirely obvious, we strongly recommend practicing this exercise in the privacy of your erotic refuge. Turn off the telephone and make any other necessary arrangements to ensure total privacy for at least an hour. Relax, play some romantic music in the background, have a glass of wine or fruit juice, and consider burning some mild incense. You should arrange for the music to play continuously for at least the next hour.

> **Sensual Suggestion**—Choose any music you find erotically stimulating. Some people are particularly turned on by hard rock, others by the Top 100 from their adolescent past, and yet others by classical concertos or experimental jazz. You may choose a set of Beatles love songs, the jazz of Tangerine Dream or Chic Corea and Return to Forever, or the "Blue Danube" by Strauss. The important thing is that the music you choose should tap into the emotional, lyrical, spontaneous part of your self.

Stand in front of the mirror and slowly remove all your clothes. As you do so, imagine that you are viewing yourself through your lover's eyes. Then, when you are completely nude, stand back from the mirror and look at your entire body from all sides. Imagine that you are an outside lover, experiencing your body from an objective point of view for the first time. As you do so, allow yourself to enjoy the feeling of rediscovering your body.

Ask yourself: "What does it feel like to live inside this body?" and "What does this body feel like from the outside to another person?" Lightly touch yourself all over, as you continue to observe yourself in the mirror, and allow yourself to experience your entire body—not just the more traditional erotic zones—as sensuous. To increase your sensitivity to this part of the exercise, you may also find it helpful to lightly massage some soothing lotion or oil into your skin from head to foot.

As a further extension of this exercise, you may wish to lie on your bed and use a hand mirror to examine certain parts of your body—particularly your genitals—more closely. As you do so, imagine how your lover must feel when he or she looks at these parts of your body in the same close-up fashion.

DAY 6

SELF-PLEASURING

If you are like most normal people interviewed by human-sexuality researchers, it may be easier for you to reach the apex of sexual ecstasy alone than in the company of another person. In fact, many sex researchers believe that you must learn to experience sexual pleasure on your own before you can reach the height of sexual fulfillment with another person.

Yet despite the so-called sexual revolution, many people experience a kind of internalized taboo against providing self-pleasuring; they simply feel uncomfortable about exploring their own sexuality without the active participation of a lover. If you are one of these people, you must get beyond these feelings to proceed with the Erotic Fulfillment Program.

Self-pleasuring is not a substitute for human contact, but in the exercise that follows we introduce the technique as a way of deepening your erotic sensitivity and your insights into your own sexual needs. It is often easier to explore your sexuality and identify your needs *without* the pressure of another person to satisfy and please.

Sensual Suggestion—Self-pleasuring can relieve stress and anxiety and help you feel good on both physical and emotional levels. This is particularly true when you are temporarily forced to be separated from your usual sexual partner. (We certainly recommend this approach in preference to simply having an outside relationship.) Furthermore, in this era of virulent sexually transmitted diseases, self-pleasuring must be considered the ultimate "safe sex." Many sex therapists also recommend self-pleasuring as a way of balancing a monogamous sexual relationship when one lover's sexual drives are more powerful than the other's, or when mitigating circumstances (such as a temporary illness or conflicting work schedules) prevent both partners from making love together as often as they might like.

Many sex therapists also recommend self-pleasuring to those who have difficulty achieving orgasms either in general, or in relation to their current sexual partner. Though exploring such issues is beyond the scope of this particular book, we do agree that getting sexually comfortable with yourself can be an excellent first step in overcoming such limitations. (Once again, if you are experiencing sexual problems, we do urge you to contact a qualified therapist who may assist you in working them out.)

As with earlier exercises, today's Erotic Fulfillment Program session should be carried out in the privacy of your erotic refuge, with the telephone turned off, at a time you are certain you won't be disturbed. Take steps to enhance the surrounding atmosphere and mood, just as if you were preparing to share this experience with your lover. Play some romantic music, pour yourself a glass of fruit juice, wine, or champagne, and take time to enjoy some sensuous and erotically stimulating foods like sorbet, fresh berries, or cheese blintzes. Take a hot bubble bath or shower to help yourself relax. If you are fortunate enough to have a fireplace in your erotic refuge, consider lighting a cozy fire, getting naked, and stretching out in front of the fireplace on the rug. In any event, you should remove all your clothes and relax in some comfortable spot.

Begin exploring the sexual sensitivity of your entire body. Remember that sexuality is not just limited to the traditional erogenous zones. What spots make you feel particularly excited when you stimulate them? Be creative, caressing your knees, ears, face, genitals, and other areas in exactly the manner that you would most like to be touched by a lover. For example, try touching yourself very lightly in various places, then more forcefully, then with light scratches, and so forth. You should also feel free to experiment with different lotions, oils, vibrators, and any other sexual aids that might help you achieve the desired sexually excited state.

Experiment with different sexual positions. For example, some people prefer to experience self-pleasuring while kneeling, others while on their sides, back, or stomach, and still others while standing in front of a full-length mirror. The point here is to do whatever it takes to make yourself feel as much sexual pleasure as you can.

As you experiment with various ways of physically stimulating your body, allow yourself the special luxury of also stimulating your mind. Have fantasies. Remember back to a time when you felt particularly connected to, and sexually excited by, a past or present lover. It is entirely natural to fantasize about someone other than your current partner. Imagine having sex with your favorite fantasy lover on the beach, under a waterfall, or in the forest. Think of specific sexual things that you enjoy—or would enjoy—doing with specific people. Imagine an oral sex festival with the new man or woman at the office. Imagine having two partners at once, or even three. Envision yourself in a pornographic film, or on the set of Lina Wertmuller's island fantasy *Swept Away*. The important thing is that you invoke the images that are most exciting to *you*.

Sensual Suggestion—As the Erotic Fulfillment Program moves forward, allow your fantasies to evolve. Images from your fantasies, after all, are part of a rich inner tapestry out of which you may create new, more scintillating scenarios in your life. Fantasy can keep you from getting into a sexual rut and help you overcome a limited mode of personal sexual expression. Even the most exotic sexual fantasies are not necessarily a sign of sexual abnormality. Consider the fact that what some people envision as exotic fantasy, others consider a normal aspect of their own real-life sexual experiences.

It is quite normal, for example, to fantasize about having sex with more than one partner, with a real-life platonic friend, with partners of the same sex as yourself, and with movie stars or other celebrity figures. It is also quite common to fantasize about having sex outdoors, on airplanes, atop the kitchen table, or in ancient palaces or caves. More exotic and unusual sexual fantasies include such scenarios as sex with animated cartoon stars (Jem and He-Man are reported favorites), sex aboard a flying saucer with visitors from outer space, and even sex with trees! Whatever your favorite sexual fantasies, it is healthy to enjoy them while experiencing self-pleasuring or any other form of sex.

Sensual Suggestion—You should, of course, consider acting out your wildest fantasies only when it is completely safe, appropriate, and possible for you to do so. If your fantasies include harming another person or if they involve children or minors, we suggest that you seek professional psychological help.

To conclude the self-pleasuring exercise, imagine that your current partner has entered the room. Now imagine telling your partner what pleases you during sex and what does not. (You might say for instance, *I prefer gentle pressure around my nipples, not powerful pressure directly on them*, or, *I like the feel of your tongue inside my thighs*. Focus, in your imagination, on those aspects of your partner's sexuality that you personally find the most exciting, and imagine yourself sexually connecting with your partner on a deep, inner level. Envision your partner doing what you ask and helping you come to climax.

After you have reached orgasm at least once through your self-pleasuring experience, continue to relax in your erotic refuge and to enjoy the physical and emotional feelings of sexual satisfaction.

Sensual Suggestion—Before you leave your erotic refuge, consider your fantasies in detail. Which fantasies would you like to incorporate into your real-life sexual experiences? Which would you like to leave in the realm of fantasy?

DAY 7

CIRCULAR MOTION

On Day 7 of the Erotic Fulfillment Program you will develop greater insight into your sexual self by drawing ''mandalas,'' ancient, circlelike figures that can enhance your ability to focus inward. Followers of Tibetan Buddhism have traditionally gazed at mandalas while meditating. And many Western psychiatrists and psychologists have had patients draw mandalas in hopes that they could resolve conflicts by projecting their feelings on the empty circular "screen." You too should find mandala drawing evocative. As you gaze at the pictures you have created, you may see the details of your life arranged in new and unusual ways. You may even find yourself expressing frustrations or desires of which you were previously unaware.

Before you actually set out to draw mandalas, read the rest of the instructions for Day 7 from beginning to end. Then, if possible, complete the exercise without referring to the text.

First, when you are certain you will have about an hour and a half of undisturbed time, prepare a few large pieces of white paper (we suggest twelve-by-eighteen-inch sheets, but any size you have handy will do), a box or crayons, paints, or pastels, and a round, dinner-size plate. Then take these materials, along with your tape recorder and the alert relaxation/music tape you made on Day 4, and retire to your erotic refuge.

For the time being, put these supplies aside. Dim the lights and play some soft music or burn some incense. Then remove your clothes and, using your favorite self-pleasuring techniques, bring yourself to sexual climax.

Once you have sexually satisfied yourself, put on some loose, flowing clothes, sit in a comfortable chair or lie on your bed, and play your alert relaxation/music tape. After you have entered the state of alert relaxation and the musical selection has begun to play, review your sexual past in your mind.

Remember your feelings about different past loves. Recall how they smelled, looked, felt, and acted. What was it like when they touched you? Is there one particular touch or gesture that really stands out in your mind? How did these past lovers talk? How did they kiss? How did they move? What did you like and what didn't you like about the way you made love together? Let your mind wander through this ancient territory for the duration of the 30-minute musical selection. Your thoughts need not be structured in any way. Instead, they should be random and flowing. Let your memories of these past relationships float in and out of your mind like sailboats moving in and out of a harbor.

After the music has ended, spend about five or ten minutes recalling any sexual dreams you may have had at various points in your life. What were the settings of these dreams, and who were your sexual partners? How did your sexual dream scenarios evolve?

How did they reflect your feelings about yourself and your life? Ask yourself, "What are my sexual dreams really like and what does this tell me about who I am at a deep sexual level?"

After you have recalled your sexual dreams, close your eyes and visualize a blank screen or a vast, endless field of snow. When your mind is blank, you will be ready for the mandala part of this exercise.

Take a sheet of paper and lay your plate on top of it. Then draw the outline of your plate with a crayon, felt-tipped marker, or paintbrush. Lift your plate and look at the circular border you have created. Now take out your drawing tools, pick a color, and draw something inside the circle. You may draw anything you like—shapes or lines, symbols, or pictures of literal people and things. The important thing is that you draw spontaneously, without analyzing or even thinking as you work. After you have produced one mandala, create three more at once.

After you have finished the mandala-drawing task, look at your drawings or simply put them aside, but *do not* take time to analyze them now. The mere creation of these pictures should provide you with a greater sense of sexual balance and harmony than you had before.

A few hours after you have produced these mandalas—or perhaps even the next day—look at them again. This time ask yourself what these drawings tell you about your inner sexual self. Turn the drawings upside down and sideways to see if any surprising features emerge.

Congratulations! You have just completed Week One of the Erotic Fulfillment Program. We suggest that you and your partner celebrate by going out for coffee, pizza, a movie, a Chinese dinner, or just a walk in the park.

WEEK ONE THE SENSUAL SELF

DAY 1 FORBIDDEN FRUIT	**DAY 2** EROTIC REFUGE	**DAY 3** INSIDE MOVES	
Pick up an orange and look at it. Notice its color, shape, and texture. Peel the orange. Hear and smell the skin being pulled apart. Eat the orange, paying full attention to all your senses.	Look around your bedroom. Study it to see whether it is conducive to the expression of your inner sexuality. Transform this environment into an erotic refuge by getting rid of clutter and reminders of former relationships; choosing soothing, sexually stimulating pictures, colors and decorations; and arranging a source of music. Choose a fantasy wardrobe to be worn when you and your partner are alone together. Transform the bathroom nearest your bedroom to make it part of your erotic refuge.	Read all Day 3 instructions twice. Have a friend record an alert relaxation induction tape. Get in a warm, soothing bath. Play the tape and, as instructed, envision warm currents of mental energy soothing each part of your body in turn. Enter the state of alert relaxation. Envision a blank white screen. Envision images of expansion and contraction.	Feel your body expanding and contracting in harmony with nature. Imagine that your body contains an inner window to all events in the natural world. Imagine that you are looking through that window and glimpsing natural scenes within your body. Return to a state of complete waking consciousness.

DAY 4 SEXUAL CENTER		DAY 5 ONE ON ONE	DAY 6 SELF- PLEASURING
Have a friend record an alert relaxation induction tape. Add 30 minutes of baroque or some other music to the tape after the induction. Go to your erotic refuge, listen to the tape, and enter the state of alert relaxation. Focus on the relationship between your innermost consciousness and your physical, sensual body throughout the duration of the musical selection. Get dressed, and as you do so continue to focus on your body.	Stand in front of your full-length mirror, gaze at your reflection, and see your inner sexuality radiating out.	Enter your erotic refuge and relax. Select and play an hour's worth of music. Stand in front of a full-length mirror, remove all your clothes, and examine your body. Imagine that you are doing so through your lover's eyes. Lightly touch yourself all over. If you want, lie on your bed and use a hand mirror to examine your genitals. Imagine how your lover feels when he or she looks at these parts of your body up close.	Go to your erotic refuge. Turn the telephone off and make sure you have complete privacy. Create a romantic mood, eat erotically stimulating food, and take a bath. Explore your body, experimenting with different sexual positions and methods of stimulation. Have erotic fantasies. Imagine telling your partner what pleases you during sex and what does not. Imagine connecting with your partner on a deep inner level. If possible, reach orgasm.

DAY 7
CIRCULAR
MOTION

Gather paper, drawing utensils, and a round dinner plate.

Retire to your erotic refuge with these materials and your alert relaxation/music tape.

Remove your clothes, dim the lights, play soft music, and use favorite self-pleasuring techniques to bring yourself to climax.

Remember past sexual relations and past sexual dreams.

Close your eyes and invoke the image of emptiness.

Trace the circular outline of your plate on a few sheets of paper.

Draw anything you like within the circles.

Put the drawings aside, then look at them later for clues to your inner sexual self.

WEEK TWO

ENTERING
THE EROTIC ZONE •

WEEK
TWO
•
E N T E R I N G
T H E   E R O T I C   Z O N E

Welcome to Week
Two of the Erotic Fulfillment Program. Now that you and your
partner have each spent some time alone getting in touch with your
individual sexual selves, it is time for you to explore your mutual
erotic potential. Week Two exercises are geared toward helping you
and your partner move beyond old sexual patterns that may inhibit
the expression of your innermost sexuality and prevent you from
growing as a couple. Your sexual growth should be greatly facilitated
as you allow rigid patterns to change. As you and your lover open
yourselves up to the new approaches suggested in Week Two, you
should learn many new things about each other and experience deepening levels of intimacy in your sexual lives.

Week Two opens with an exercise called "First Communion,"
in which you and your partner will begin to talk about your personal
sexuality more honestly than you ever have before. Once you have
initiated this deeper level of intimate communication, you will get
in touch with each other's sensual side by working out. The physical
exercises you do together will help you key in to your sensual selves.

You will continue to explore the wild side through innovative
massage techniques, a scratching and biting exercise, and even the
creative use of sexual cries and whispers and "sex toys" that can
be easily created from common objects. The week will culminate as
you learn to induce the profound experience of a shared, or mutual,
dream, in which you both dream about the same type of experience
at the same time. When you and your lover learn to induce shared

dreams at will, the impact should be profound. Not only should you be able to explore various aspects of your relationship on a deeper level, you should also deepen your emotional and sexual bond.

After you and your partner have completed the Week Two exercises, you should be more intimately connected—and more knowledgeable about each other's sexuality—than you were before. The mood will be set for Week Three of the Erotic Fulfillment Program, in which you and your lover will learn to merge your essential selves and experience the world through each other's eyes.

DAY 8

FIRST COMMUNION

Today you will shift your focus from yourself to your lover and your sexual relationship. Your goal on Day 8, and for the duration of the Erotic Fulfillment Program: enhancing the *interpersonal* intuitive skills that should take you and your lover to a higher, more intimate sexual plane. To help you along, we introduce a technique we call "communion," in which you communicate with your partner in an open, totally honest way. By sharing your feelings on life and sex—and learning to trust one another with these feelings—you will enhance your mutual intimacy and your rapport.

Sensual Suggestion—While the Erotic Fulfillment Program contains two communion exercises, you and your partner may want to hold communion every week at a regular time. You may also find it valuable to use this technique as a weekly communication tool long after you have completed the 30-day program.

To hold your first communion, retire to your erotic refuge with your partner at a time when you feel you will have at least an hour without being disturbed. Then change into loose, flowing clothes and share some fresh fruit, cheese, or wine. Before you begin your actual talk, we would like you to remember to tell the truth, to listen carefully to your partner, and to be supportive of what he or she says, no matter what that might be. Please do not make your lover feel guilty for any thoughts or feelings, and try to avoid feelings of guilt yourself. As you speak, look into your partner's eyes.

Once you have absorbed these suggestions, we would like you to address the issues below, in order. After you have both given your answers, each must try to respond to what the other has said. Remember, this is not the time to be judgmental. No matter what your partner tells you, be as loving and accepting as you can.

- When did you have your first orgasm? Was it with or without another person present?

- What was your first *positive* sexual experience?

- What are your earliest memories about sex?

- What were your earliest sexual fantasies?

- What role do these early memories and fantasies play in your sex life today?

Sensual Suggestion—After you have held your first communion, take some time to gently make love.

DAY 9

WORKING OUT

Begin Day 9 by participating in an overtly phys-ical, but not overtly sexual, athletic activity with your lover. Go to a health club and work out on Nautilus equipment, ride bicycles, climb a cliff, row a boat, go swimming or scuba diving, practice aerobics or aikido, go running, or just go hiking or for a long brisk walk. (Of course, any activity you choose should be one that is well suited to your current level of athletic experience and physical con-dition.)

As you enjoy your chosen activity together, notice the way that your lover relates to his or her body. How does your partner move?

What about those movements do you find attractive and sexually stimulating? Note your lover's changing facial expressions, as well as the look and smell of your lover's hair and skin. Continue with this first part of today's exercise for at least two or three hours.

When you return home, take a shower with your lover, but don't make love just yet. Instead, just enjoy the overall feeling of one another's body as you cover each other with soap, and shampoo and rinse each other's hair. Be certain to use a fresh bar of unscented soap, as well as an unscented shampoo.

> **Sensual Suggestion**—An important aspect of Inner Sex is reactivating all your senses, including your sense of smell. We therefore suggest that you deliberately avoid heavily scented cleaning products, cosmetics, perfumes, colognes, and deodorants, at least for the duration of the Erotic Fulfillment Program. At a very basic level, human beings are undeniably animals. There is nothing more stimulating to the sexual/animal side of our nature than the natural scents of a clean—but not overly sanitized or deodorized—human body. As long as you are clean, it is better to smell like a wild animal than an artificial chemical concoction manufactured in a factory.

When you complete your shower, you and your lover should towel each other off, then slip into some of the comfortable clothes you selected during Week One. Again, avoid splashing on any colognes or perfumes.

Now enter the kitchen with your lover, and prepare a sensuous meal to be shared in your erotic refuge. Make the meal light, but as stimulating to all of your senses as possible. The meal might include, for example, such special treats as poached salmon, Caesar salad, fresh imported vegetables, and citrus fruit. You should avoid drinking alcohol for this exercise, since mixing alcohol with interpersonal sexual activity is very much like soaking the kindling in water before lighting a fire.

Do not taste the food while it is being prepared, but wait until you and your lover are ready to share it in your erotic refuge. After you enter this special place, put on some music and turn off or disconnect the phone, in general making sure the two of you will not be disturbed. Eat in moderation—not until you are full, but only until you have taken the edge off your hunger.

> ***Sensual Suggestion***—Notice that eating, like lovemaking, can be a highly erotic experience. For a particularly vivid exploration of the intimate relationship between food and sex, try checking out the video of the intensely sexual film, *9½ Weeks*.

Extract the most from this shared meal. Enjoy it by candlelight, for instance, and allow yourself to experience it as a prelude to the lovemaking session to follow.

When you have completed your meal, you and your lover should forget about the dishes for now and just place them aside without leaving the room. Then you should both stand up and slowly undress each other, touching each other's body gently all over as you begin moving toward making love. Before rushing madly toward the most sensitive sexual parts of your lover's body—clitoris, breasts, penis, for example—first caress other erotic zones such as—in women— the hands, neck, back, thighs, behind the ears, around the waist; and—in men—the chest and nipples, the buttocks, and the inside of the thighs.

You and your lover should also focus on getting to know each other's sexual scents as an aspect of foreplay before making love. Take time to get in touch with the smell of your lover's hair, skin, and genitals.

As you touch your lover's body in sexual ways, remember how he or she looked while involved in athletic activities earlier in the day. Consider, now, what these activities tell you about your lover's inner relationship to his or her own body. Without overanalyzing your impressions, ask yourself if they suggest or inspire any special sexual action on your part. If so, go ahead and sexually stimulate your lover in that special way. Did you notice your lover flexing a particular muscle or taking special pleasure in thoroughly working a certain part of his or her body? If so, apply focused tactile stim- ulation to those places now. Closely observe your lover's response, then gently adjust your own activities and movements in the appro- priate way.

Finally, as you naturally move into making love, you and your partner should make contact from head to toe, keeping both your hands flowing, and touching as many points along your bodies as you can throughout the entire experience. After making love, keep touching each other with your hands until you are both feeling tired and ready to go to sleep.

DAY 10

MYSTIC MASSAGE

On Day 10, you will use the alert relaxation technique to help you give and receive a highly erotic massage. Before you begin, make sure you have your alert relaxation/music tape and your cassette recorder handy. Then retire to your erotic refuge with your partner and remove your clothes. Disconnect or turn off your phone and make sure you will not be disturbed in any way.

> **Sensual Suggestion**—If you want, turn up the thermostat to make sure you will be completely comfortable without clothes or covers.

> **Sensual Suggestion**—For a wonderful variation during this exercise, you might want to replace the music part of your relaxation tape with a recording of such environmental sound effects as ocean waves, rain, or birds.

> **Sensual Suggestion**—We urge you and your partner to take time to check out one of the many excellent video explorations of sensuous massage techniques available at video stores before beginning today's session. We specifically recommend *The Art of Sensuous Massage* and *Secrets of Euromassage*, though many other tapes are excellent as well. There are also many excellent illustrated books that describe a variety of massage techniques—though we personally prefer the videotapes for their unparalleled manner and level of presentation. These resources provide extensive instruction in specific massage techniques that are beyond the scope of our discussion.

Now decide which of you will be the first to receive a sensuous, full-body massage. (After one of you has had a chance to be the receptive partner, you will both take a break, then reverse roles.)

When you are the partner receiving the massage, begin by lying facedown on the bed and taking a deep breath. As your lover begins massaging your body, focus on entering the state of alert relaxation.

> **Sensual Suggestion**—By now, many Inner Sex participants may be able to enter the state of alert relaxation without the induction tape,

simply by visualizing warm currents moving from muscle to muscle throughout the body. If the person receiving the massage has this capability, simply have him or her induce a state of alert relaxation, then begin to play the music part of the tape. If the individual to receive the massage prefers, however, play the whole tape and begin the massage when the music (or the environmental sound effects) begins.

As you feel yourself moving into the altered state of alert relaxation, imagine, as you did during Week One, that your body is a window through which you may envision many distant natural environments. Begin by imagining rivers and streams, hills and valleys, fields and trees, all viewed through the window of your body.

Now allow this inner scenery to expand and contract in your mind's eye. For instance, see the streams expanding into lakes, rivers, and eventually, into vast rolling oceans. Then see the oceans contracting once more to rivers, lakes, streams, and eventually, to drops of rain. Watch the hills becoming mountains, then, once again, becoming hills. See the valleys becoming vast canyons, then going in reverse, from canyons to valleys to narrow ravines. See the fields and trees becoming vast, open forests, then contracting once more to fields, meadows, and tiny patches of grass. Allow your deepest emotions to ebb and flow with the changing scenery in your body. Allow your inner scenery to ebb and flow with the changing sensations of the massage.

Complete today's exercise by lying beside your partner on the bed or carpet. Hold one another and synchronize your breathing. Then enjoy the deep sense of closeness created by this experience.

When you are the active partner, you should provide your lover with a deeply relaxing massage for at least 30 minutes. You and your partner should deliberately avoid verbal communication during this experience and, instead, communicate via direct physical contact and the emotional resonance that the contact generates. As you will no doubt discover, massage not only relaxes the body, but the mind as well. It can help create the emotional setting for a deep, inner communication that enhances your ability to intuit your partner's needs and desires while making love.

As you massage your partner, concentrate on creating sensations of balance in his or her body. As you did yesterday, focus on touching your partner's body in ways that you intuitively sense will feel the best. Make long, deep, and confident movements with both hands. Use warm, unscented oil or lotion. And vary the manner and intensity of your stokes. After you have massaged the back of your partner's body for at least 15 minutes, gently encourage him or her to turn over by slipping a hand under a shoulder. Then complete the massage with your partner lying on his or her back.

After you have both received a massage, lie beside each other on the bed or carpet. Hold one another and synchronize your breathing. If you want to, now is the time to make love. If you are both too deeply relaxed or tired for full sexual intercourse, however, just enjoy the deep sense of closeness created by this experience.

DAY 11

LOVE BITES

On Day 11 you will use a biting and scratching technique to explore the highly erotic boundary between pleasure and pain. Please understand, we by no means advocate that you or your partner hurt each other in any way. But today's technique will enable the two of you to explore the limits of the *pleasurable* pressure you may apply to the various parts of each other's bodies.

Begin by joining one another for a sensuous bath or shower. Take time to luxuriate in this experience: burn incense, play music, even illuminate the room with candles or red or pink light bulbs. Cover one another's bodies all over with fresh-smelling soap, and wash each other's hair with an unscented or lightly scented, very sudsy shampoo. Don't just pour the shampoo in and rinse it out, but use it as an excuse to give your lover a soothing scalp massage. And don't just pass around the soap, but use it to cover every inch of your lover's body.

After you have completed your shower or bath, retire to the bedroom of your erotic refuge and enjoy a light, sensuous meal. Both you and your lover should be completely naked for this experience, so make certain that the room temperature is comfortable before you begin.

Begin by sitting directly across from one another and consciously synchronizing your breathing. As you do so, concentrate on entering a mutually harmonious mood in which all outside concerns fade from your immediate awareness. Then, reach over and very lightly scratch your partner's skin with the tips of your nails, so that his or her hair bristles and goose bumps form. Allow your partner to do the same to you.

Continue this activity for as long as it feels pleasurable for both of you, gradually progressing from light scratches to slightly stronger scratches over the surface of your skin. Tell each other where the scratches feel good and where they do not. For each body area, communicate the intensity of the scratch that feels best.

After you have finished scratching each other, bite each other in much the same way. Lightly bite your partner's skin, glancing your teeth across the surface so that his or her hair bristles and goose bumps form. Allow your partner to do the same to you.

Continue this activity for as long as it feels pleasurable for both of you, gradually progressing from light bites to increasingly stronger bites over the surface of your skin. (Don't ever bite so hard, however, that you actually hurt your partner.) Tell each other where the bites feel good and where they do not. For each body area, communicate the intensity of the bite that feels best, perhaps using a scale of intensity from "no reaction" at 1 to a "superbly intense reaction" at 5.

Finally, using the information you have learned from this controlled biting and scratching, bite and scratch each other in an increasingly spontaneous way. Playfully nibble at one another's ears and necks. Gently scratch each other's buttocks, chest, and thighs.

Engage in this stimulating form of sexual foreplay for as long as you can without actually making love. As you bite and scratch, attempt to tune in to each other's bodies on a basic physical level. Also attempt to understand the deep emotional tenor of your lover based on his or her response to pleasure and pain. Finally, when you can no longer hold back, allow yourself to make love in a spontaneous and passionate way.

Consider, if you will, that those parts of your lover's body that can be bitten or scratched can also be kissed. Complete this exercise by lying in one another's arms and quietly kissing some of the same areas you have recently bitten or scratched.

DAY 12

CRIES AND WHISPERS

On Day 12 of the Erotic Fulfillment Program you will start by focusing on the sounds of the natural world. To begin today's exercise, you and your lover should go together to some easily accessible location in which you can both feel a sense of closeness to nature. You might choose a spot under a favorite tree in your backyard, a rooftop garden, an apple orchard, a picnic ground, or a beach. If it is particularly cold or otherwise treacherous outdoors, you may substitute a spot from which you can observe nature in comfort: a rustic country lodge or the portal of a boat in dock will do.

Take some time to let go of the stresses of your everyday life and enjoy your surroundings. As you do so, pay close attention to the sounds of nature. Can you hear sea gulls calling as they circle overhead? Is the wind blowing through nearby branches? Is rain or sleet or even hail pounding the surface of your window? Is water gently lapping the shore at the edge of your favorite lake or pond? Allow these sounds to fill your senses, stimulating feelings of closeness to nature, and to your lover as well.

Pay attention to the sounds you and your lover make in relation to one another and your environment. Listen to each other's footsteps crunching over dried leaves, and the sounds of your own and your lover's breathing. Notice any other sounds that each of you make in the normal course of your activities, such as those you make while tearing the wrapper off a candy bar, zipping your jacket, or brushing crumbs off your jeans. Listen to the sounds you make in conversation, momentarily imagining your spoken words strictly as sounds in and of themselves.

After you have completed this first phase of today's exercise, return to your erotic refuge with your lover for a session of making love.

Sensual Suggestion—For today's exercise, don't play music in the background. We also suggest that, providing the ventilation is adequate, you close the window of your room so that stray or extraneous sounds don't filter in. If possible, it would be best not to use an air conditioner or fan.

After you enter your erotic refuge and create as quiet an atmosphere as is comfortably possible, take off your clothes and sit across from each other. Then, synchronize your breathing with that of your lover. As you breathe together, notice the silent rhythms and sounds of your breath. After a while, you might both even want to exaggerate your breathing sounds, though you shouldn't get carried away. In our opinion, hyperventilation—and the resulting projectile vomiting—is not an especially erotic experience. Continue to synchronize your breathing with one another until you find yourselves gradually and naturally making the transition into lovemaking.

As you and your partner make love, focus on the sounds generated by this sexual encounter. Does the rate and tenor of your breathing change and become more pronounced? Do you become quieter than usual, or do your passionate cries of ecstasy filter through the wall and startle or even scare your next-door neighbors? Do the sounds made by your partner while making love correspond to the deepest feelings you have about him or her in general? Do the sounds made by both of you relate to the specific, physical feelings you are having while making love?

As you listen to your lover, notice how the sounds he or she makes express feelings on a profound inner level. Notice how the sounds ebb and flow from moment to moment, right along with the feelings themselves. Then allow yourself to respond directly to those feelings on a deep, intuitive level, without analyzing or even thinking about the sounds.

Finally, throughout the course of this lovemaking session, you and your lover should make a special point of deliberately expressing your feelings to one another through sound. You can take this aspect of today's exercise as far as feels comfortable for both of you, while also experimenting to see what works. Instead of communicating in words, allow yourselves to communicate in cries and whispers. If your lover touches you in an especially erotic fashion, allow yourself the pleasure of moaning in response to the touch. When you touch your lover in some similarly erotic fashion, signal your enjoyment through a throaty rumble or purr. If you feel inhibited by the animal or guttural sounds of sex, now is the time to let those inhibitions fade. As your lovemaking session continues, we suggest that you become increasingly voluble, increasingly expressive and instinctive. By listening to the sounds you both make while making love, and by expressing yourselves in a completely nonlinguistic fashion, you should find yourselves experiencing a deepened, intuitive sexual connection.

DAY 13

OBJECTS OF DESIRE

In contrast with many of the more controlled or internalized exercises of the past week and a half, Day 13 should provide you and your lover with an opportunity for a more free-wheeling, primarily physical, exploration.

To practice the exercise for Day 13, first collect a few objects that might make sex more exciting or fun and bring them into your erotic refuge. We suggest such erotic toys and aids as feathers and straws, colorful scarves and beads, a water atomizer, bottles of natural oil, jars of jelly or gourmet preserves, fake fur mittens, garters, cotton swabs, hand-held mirrors, spiked high-heeled shoes, fine paintbrushes, flowers, and even flashlights.

> **Sensual Suggestion**—If you and your partner are so inclined, you might take some time to visit one or two shops that specialize in sexual aids such as vibrators, lotions, and rubber goods. You might also look through a mail order catalog featuring a variety of sexual aids recommended and approved by the Institute for Advanced Study of Human Sexuality, a research facility and graduate school offering state-approved degrees in human sexuality. To obtain the catalog, write to the Institute at 1523 Franklin Street, San Francisco, California 94109.

Remember, use your imagination. As long as an object appeals to you, is not dangerous, and will not strain your relationship, it is fair game. For example, you might simply enjoy lightly tickling your partner in various erogenous zones with a flower, a feather, a fake fur mitten, or a moistened cotton swab. (Try lightly stimulating your partner's clitoris with a cotton swab moistened with hand lotion or oil.) Some people prefer the feeling of leather or terry cloth to the feeling of fur or cotton, so feel free to explore those textures and materials that feel the best to you and your lover.

Regardless of the particular toys that you and your partner choose to employ, the point of today's exercise is sharing the highly erotic experience of crossing certain sexual lines together, in the secure and healthy context of an intimate, intuitive relationship.

Once you have chosen your special objects, retire to your erotic refuge and use your instincts. You may, of course, play music, burn incense, or follow any of the Erotic Fulfillment Program techniques you truly enjoy. But most of all, use your imagination. This is not the time for explicit instructions from us.

DAY 14

DREAM WEAVERS

One of the most profound experiences you can share with your sexual partner is what we call a "mutual dream," in which you both dream the same type of thing at the same time. The ability to have mutual dreams can create feelings of deep inner communion, almost as if you and your partner have been together in an alternate reality or have shared an inexplicable "psychic" experience.

Of course, the explanation for shared dreams is really much more straightforward. Since dreams are so directly influenced by experiences in the waking world, two people who have many waking experiences in common are also eventually likely to share the general content or subject matter of at least some of their dreams. This is especially true when the individuals involved are sexual partners.

When you and your lover learn to induce shared dreams at will, the impact can be profound. Not only should you be able to explore various aspects of your relationship on a deeper level, you should also deepen your emotional and sexual bond.

To share a dream with your partner tonight, begin early in the day by swapping some clothes or other personal articles. Scarves, hats, gloves, coats, sweaters, and even underwear would work well. If you are both in the habit of wearing cologne, now is the time to exchange scents. Spend as much time as you possibly can with your lover today, aiming for a setting rich in sensory and emotional stimulation. If you are both working today, try to meet for lunch or at least dinner. You may also just go out to a sensually provocative movie. We do not suggest that you see a pornographic film, but rather, one that tells a charged or exciting romantic tale. *Wuthering Heights* or *Gone With the Wind* would work well, as would *Choose Me, Love Scenes, Castaway, Two Moon Junction*, and *Annie Hall*. If moviegoing is your choice, we also suggest that you see this movie in some atmospheric section of town. Greenwich Village in New York City, Westwood Village in Los Angeles, or Harvard Square in Cambridge, Massachusetts, would be appropriate areas. You might also stop for some coffee or cheese and wine. For this exercise, make sure to avoid theaters in suburban multiplexes or malls. We also suggest that you enhance this experience—and your mutual intimacy—by discussing the positive aspects of your relationship or some concerns in your separate lives. Remember, during the time you spend together, to periodically remind each other that you plan to include elements of this shared experience in tonight's dreams.

Sometime in the course of your shared activity, you and your lover should each select a special, symbolic object from the immediate environment. The object should represent some romantic aspect of the time you have spent together during the day.

If possible, arrive home from your shared activity in the evening shortly before you plan to retire to bed for the night. Then go directly to your erotic refuge with the intent of making love. You may burn incense, play music, or massage or even gently bite and scratch each other. Use some of the sexual objects you explored yesterday, and do whatever else you can to arouse and satisfy each other and to become emotionally and physically close.

Then, before actually going to sleep, both you and your partner should exchange the symbolic objects you found or bought during the day. Hold and touch your objects and think, for a few moments, about the day you have both just spent. Envision what you did today, during your shared experience. And especially picture explicit details of the time you spent making love. Then, put your symbolic objects down by your bed and tell yourselves, *Tonight, we will share part of our dreams*. You should each also tell yourself: *In the morning, when I wake up, I will recall my dreams*. Gently let go of this second thought the moment you form it. Then, as you and your partner drift off to sleep, envision your dream objects and let the events of the day and images of your lovemaking float gently through your minds.

> **Sensual Suggestion**—When you wake up, the first thing you should do is focus on recalling your dreams. To retain your dreams as completely as possible, you must first understand that dream memories may be as fleeting as your next breath of air. Therefore, whenever you start to wake up, be it the middle of the night or first thing in the morning, do not open your eyes or even move. Instead, stop and focus entirely on recalling your dreams. Don't pressure yourself to remember detailed dream descriptions in exact chronological order. Instead, lie still and allow your dream memories to emerge gradually and spontaneously into your waking consciousness.

After you and your lover have had this quiet time and are both fully awake, compare notes. How similar or different were your dreams? Did you dream about each other? Did you experience a bona fide *shared* dream, in which the details conjured by each of you were startlingly alike? Were there sexual components to your dreams?

> **Sensual Suggestion**—We suggest that you and your partner attempt to induce shared dreams a few times a week for the duration of the Erotic Fulfillment Program. We would also like you to continue the dream recollection techniques we introduced today. You and your partner should find your intimacy increasing if you discuss the content of your dreams on a regular basis.

WEEK TWO   ENTERING THE EROTIC ZONE

DAY 8 FIRST COMMUNION	**DAY 9** WORKING OUT	**DAY 10** MYSTIC MASSAGE	
Retire to your erotic refuge with your partner.	Participate in an athletic activity with your partner.	Retire to your erotic refuge with your partner.	The recipient should also allow this inner scenery—and his or her deepest emotions—to ebb and flow with the massage. Lie on one side for 15 minutes, then turn over and lie on the other side for another 15 minutes. Trade places. After you have both had a massage, lie together, synchronize your breathing, and make love if desired.
Change into loose clothes and share some fresh fruit, cheese, or wine. Remember to be honest, attentive, and nonjudgmental. Guided by the Day 8 questions, discuss your feelings about sex with your partner.	Subtly observe your lover during this activity. Go home and take a shower with your lover. Prepare and eat a sensuous meal. Touch each other in sexual ways, recall the day's activities, and make love.	Decide which one will receive a massage first. The person receiving the massage should enter the state of alert relaxation. The person giving the massage should focus on creating a sense of balance in his or her partner's body. The one being massaged should imagine that his or her body contains a portal through which it is possible to see distant natural environments.	

DAY 11 LOVE BITES	**DAY 12** CRIES AND WHISPERS		**DAY 13** OBJECTS OF DESIRE
Take a bath or shower with your partner.	Visit a spot of natural beauty with your partner.	Make love, and as you do so, focus on the sounds generated by your sexual encounter. Express your feelings through sound.	Collect some objects that you feel will enhance your enjoyment of sex.
Eat a light, sensuous meal together in your erotic refuge.	Pay attention to the sounds of nature.		Retire to your erotic refuge.
Sit directly across from one another and synchronize your breathing.	Listen to the sounds you and your lover make as you experience this natural environment.		Use your instincts, and explore what feels best for you and your partner.
Lightly scratch each other's skin with your nails. Experiment with scratches until you learn where, if anywhere, they feel best.	Return to your erotic refuge, take off your clothes, and synchronize your breathing with that of your lover.		
Lightly bite each other's skin, experimenting with that technique as well.	Notice the rhythms and sounds of your breath.		
Make love in a spontaneous and passionate way.			

DAY 14
DREAM
WEAVERS

Before you and
your partner go
off to start the
day, swap
some clothes
or other per-
sonal articles.

Later on, meet
for lunch or
dinner.

If you like, see
a sensually
provocative—
but not porno-
graphic—
movie.

Select a sym-
bolic object as
a souvenir
from the im-
mediate envi-
ronment of the
theater or res-
taurant.

Go home, re-
tire to your
erotic refuge,
and make love.

Before falling
asleep, ex-
change sym-
bolic objects.

Hold the ob-
jects and con-
sider the day
you have just
had.

Put your sym-
bolic objects
down, and
vow to share
part of your
dreams.

Drift off to
sleep.

When you
wake up in
the morning,
describe your
dreams to each
other.

WEEK THREE

INTUITIVE SEX

WEEK THREE

•

I N T U I T I V E
S E X

Communication, as you no doubt realize by now, is the key to the deepest form of Inner Sex. Week Three is all about communication—communication so intense and all-encompassing that you and your lover may almost seem to read each other's minds. The route to this profound inner communication is a technique we call transpersonal focusing, in which you and your partner envision yourselves trading places. In the course of the transpersonal focusing exercises that follow, your sense of separation from your partner should blur as your comprehension of his or her inner self evolves and expands.

Before you actually begin the intense transpersonal focusing exercises of Week Three, you will take a break from the erotic sensitivity exercises of the past week. In our first Week Three exercise, "Fortress of Solitude," you will take some time to get back in touch with the mundane details of your everyday life and reestablish some personal space. After you have had a day to yourself, the transpersonal phase of the Erotic Fulfillment Program can begin.

The transpersonal exercises take you on a journey of mutual exploration one step at a time. In the first of these exercises— "Mirroring"—you and your partner will study each other's deepest sexual desires through the art of pantomime. In the next two transpersonal focusing exercises you will learn to merge your identities, ultimately reaching orgasm while mentally trading bodies and envisioning the world through each other's eyes. In the course of Week Three, you will also explore the realm of androgyny, getting more closely in touch with the feminine and masculine characteristics that form your true sexual self. You will also focus on freeing yourself of sexual stereotypes that may have kept you trapped in an erotic rut. Toward that end, you will even imagine yourself and your lover in the form of wild animals while making love.

These potent transpersonal techniques form the core of our Erotic Fulfillment Program. For understanding each other on this deep inner level is sure to enhance your sexual intimacy and enable you to tune in more precisely to each other's innermost erotic desires and needs. Indeed, it is worth considering a statistic often quoted by human sexuality researchers: Less than 50 percent of the married, hetero-sexual women interviewed in a recent study reportedly experienced orgasms on a regular basis. On the other hand, 95 percent of the lesbian couples interviewed in this study could reach climax again and again. We are willing to consider the possibility, therefore, that many couples experience a lack of sexual fulfillment because of a simple lack of familiarity with one another's minds and bodies. Our transpersonal focusing exercises should help you overcome these barriers by literally helping you to see the world, for a while, at least, from your lover's point of view.

We want to point out that the transpersonal focusing exercises of Week Three may be extremely vivid and intense. It is crucial, therefore, that you not carry out these exercises while drinking al-cohol or while under the influence of psychoactive or so-called rec-reational drugs. You should also avoid these exercises if either you or your partner feel at all uncomfortable with what we're suggesting, or if either of you begin to feel uneasy at any point. If you or your lover have any psychiatric problems, you should consider avoiding these exercises until you have had a chance to discuss them with a competant therapist or psychiatrist.

You will conclude Week Three with an intense form of Inner Sex that can be achieved through the induction of lucid dreams—dreams in which you know you are dreaming *while the dream is in progress*. As you master the technique, you and your partner will see yourselves meeting up in your mutual lucid dreams. And, without any worldly restrictions whatsoever, you should be able to make unbridled love in your dreams.

Finally, Week Three is a good time to share with your partner any remaining sexual requests that you have not previously discussed.

DAY 15

FORTRESS OF SOLITUDE

By this point in the Erotic Fulfillment Program, you may be experiencing a desire for some private, personal space. We therefore recommend that you take this opportunity to recharge and increase your sexual energy by experiencing a day and night of relative solitude and absolute sexual abstinence.

Begin by spending at least a couple of hours away from your lover. If possible, take a walk in some natural setting such as a park, beach, botanical garden, or forest. If that is extremely inconvenient, take a leisurely walk around a nearby neighborhood or town. If the weather is poor, you may also simply visit a few art galleries or your natural history museum or even a downtown department store with fine clothes and elaborate displays. Remember, since both you and your lover will be practicing this exercise today, you should either go to separate locations or to the same location at different times of the day.

> *Sensual Suggestion*—If you decide to carry out the first part of this exercise in a museum, city center, or store, where you are bound to see other people, remember the enormous potential for anonymity and solitude in a crowd.

As you visit your chosen place, enjoy the luxury of being alone. Let the sense of tranquillity so often generated by solitude seep in. If you have chosen natural surroundings like a park or beach, enjoy the sense of gentle symmetry and peace. Allow the environment to stimulate you on as many different sensory levels as possible. If you have chosen a populated urban area, notice how soothing it is to get lost in the milling anonymity of a crowd. Pay attention to the smell of the atmosphere, the sound of the wind blowing through leaves, the murmur of voices, or the feeling of sand or grass under your feet and the color of the sky. Notice the architectural style of buildings, as well as the colors and textures in paintings, exhibits, or clothing. If other people are around you, notice their facial expressions and movements in the context of their environment. Relish the taste of any special foods—cotton candy, soft pretzels, fresh apples, cheese danishes—available in or around your immediate environment. Take time to enjoy the overall feeling of your body. Notice the way it stretches; the way it breathes and sweats when you move at a faster pace; and especially, the way you feel at a deep, sexual level given your experiences of the past 14 days.

Continue to maintain this focus for at least half an hour. Then, take some time to focus on your innermost emotional and sexual feelings toward your lover. Think about all the ways in which your life has changed since your partner became a significant part of it. Remember what your life was like before you met, and imagine what it might be like now, had you never gotten together.

Tonight, when you return home, enter your erotic refuge *by yourself*, and induce a state of alert relaxation. (You may do this simply by visualizing currents of warm energy passing through your body, or you may use your alert relaxation/music tape.) As you become more and more relaxed, imagine that your lover is there with you and see the sorts of detailed, sexual things you would be doing if you were both together. Let pictures run through your mind in explicit detail. No matter how sexually aroused you may be feeling at this point, however, do not directly stimulate yourself sexually or allow yourself to have an orgasm if this can be avoided.

If you and your lover share the same erotic refuge at all times, arrange to practice the final phase of this exercise during different times. We also suggest that, if you live with your lover, you plan to spend tonight in separate rooms. If that is not possible, simply sleep in your clothes.

> **Sensual Suggestion**—If you and your lover arrange to practice the final phase of this exercise simultaneously, from physically distant locations, you will have an opportunity to explore the potentially powerful sensation of forming an intuitive sexual connection while physically separated. For the greatest effect, avoid planning specific sexual imagery with your partner and see what spontaneously emerges. Later, when you get back together, you can compare your experiences.

DAY 16

MIRRORING

Even when you and your lover have been together for years, it isn't always easy to verbally express your most intimate sexual needs and desires. It may be especially difficult for you both to do so when you've been together for some lesser period of time. Although your sexual relationship may bring you and your partner into the closest conceivable physical contact, there may still be aspects of your innermost sexuality that you find yourself holding back.

During Day 16 you will move through some of these barriers by gently communicating your sexual feelings *without* explaining yourself in words. Our exercise, called "Mirroring," is based in part on method acting as first introduced by the great acting teacher, Stanislavsky, and in part on an adaptation of that technique as suggested by Robert Lawlor, author of *Earth Honoring: The New Male Sexuality*.

To start the charades exercise, you and your lover should retire to your erotic refuge sometime when you will have at least an hour to yourselves. Of course, you may play music—we suggest music without lyrics—burn incense, or do whatever else you like to make yourselves feel at ease.

Remove your clothes and sit across from each other on the bed or on a soft carpet on the floor. You will then take turns playacting or simply touching one another. Your goal: to communicate your deepest feelings and desires without the need to express them in words.

One of you must go first. To do so, take a few seconds to consider a desired but hard-to-express sexual fantasy or act (including just a simple touch, if that is what you have in mind) that you would like to communicate to your partner. Close your eyes and see the desired scene in your mind's eye. Picture it as intensely as possible, until you feel as though you are *there*. Then open your eyes and act out the scene for your lover.

For instance, if you desire to be touched under your buttocks or over the surface of your chest, touch your lover there now. Touch your lover not only in the exact spot where you would like to be touched in return, but also in exactly the same fashion. If you desire to make love in a standing position, in the bathtub, or in leather and chains, demonstrate that to your lover now.

After you have demonstrated your desires through your movements, your lover should mirror those movements in a sort of pantomime or slow-motion erotic dance. If your lover does not return the gesture or movement you meant to communicate, simply communicate your wishes—nonverbally, of course—again. Avoid any facial or other expressions of displeasure, repeating the gesture calmly, as an act of nonjudgmental sexual communication. When your lover returns your gesture in a way that looks or feels pleasurable to you, continue to move with your partner in unison.

After you and your partner have moved together for a while, switch roles. In essence, you will be taking turns mirroring one another's movements, gradually allowing the flow of those movements to become more and more erotic. You should avoid communicating verbally until this exercise is over.

As your mirroring gestures become more and more erotically stimulating, and you feel yourselves becoming sexually aroused, discontinue the mirroring phase of this exercise. Instead, place your lover's hand lightly over your own. Then, with your lover's hand resting upon and following yours, touch yourself in the most erotically sensitive parts of your body in exactly the manner that you most want to be touched. After a few minutes of this activity, reverse the positions of your hands, allowing your partner to touch you directly while you guide his or her hand with yours. Finally, remove your hand altogether and allow your lover to touch you without further guidance.

Then switch roles.

Sensual Suggestion—You and your lover may wish to add the latter phase of this mirroring exercise to the regular repertoire of your love-making sessions. Sometimes a little direct intervention can have a remarkably positive influence on facilitating intuition.

Of course, you may complete the mirroring technique by making love.

DAY 17

TRANSPERSONAL FOCUSING

On Day 17 you will extend yesterday's mirroring exercise by focusing your imagination on what it feels like to be inside your lover's body and mind. To facilitate this process, you will use a technique we call *transpersonal focusing*, in which two people envision themselves literally trading places. (For extensive exercises using this technique, please see our companion volume, *Mystical Experiences in 30 Days: The Higher Consciousness Program*.)

Sensual Suggestion—Do not, under any circumstances, carry out this exercise or the three that follow while drinking alcohol or while under the influence of psychoactive or so-called recreational drugs. You should also avoid these exercises if either you or your partner feel at all uncomfortable with what we're suggesting, or if either of you begin to feel uneasy at any point. If you or your lover have any psychiatric problems, you should consider avoiding these exercises until you have had a chance to discuss them with a competent therapist or psychiatrist.

Before you begin today's exercise, prepare a plate of fresh fruit and cheese and stock your erotic refuge with the music you enjoy most. Also make sure you have a candle, a candle holder, and some matches. Make sure to disconnect your phone and, in general, arrange to be undisturbed for at least 45 minutes.

Once you have retired to your special room, turn up the thermostat so that you will be completely comfortable in the nude. Then take off your clothes and sit on the floor facing your lover. Turn the lights down, light the candle, and place it between you. Remember, try to avoid conversation until the exercise is complete.

When you are ready, notice your partner's breathing and your own for 3 or 4 minutes. After a while, inhale and exhale in synchrony with your partner. As you do so, look deeply into one another's eyes.

As you look into your lover's eyes, imagine that they are yours. Further imagine that you are sitting in your lover's position, looking back through his or her eyes into your own. Then shift your focus back so that you see yourself once more looking into your lover's eyes from your original perspective. Continue shifting your focus back and forth in this fashion until you can almost imagine yourself occupying both positions at once.

Continue to synchronize your breathing and to maintain this focus until you momentarily feel as though any feelings of separation between you and your lover have dissolved.

Now imagine that your partner is not a separate and distinct individual, but is, instead, just another aspect of your own existence. Look deeply into your lover's eyes and say to yourself, "My lover is another aspect of myself." Repeat this sentence several times in your thoughts until you feel its deeper meaning sink in.

When you sense a deepening feeling of connectedness between you, imagine what it feels like to experience reality from within your lover's body. Focus your thoughts especially on your lover's sexual feelings as you envision yourself experiencing them from your lover's perspective. At the same time, continue to maintain an equal focus on your own mental and physical existence.

You and your partner may communicate the fact that you have each completed this portion of the exercise by closing your eyes and lowering your heads. When you've both finished, close your eyes and allow your breathing to return to normal. Gradually reassimilate your sense of yourself as a separate individual. When you feel that you have regained a sense of equilibrium, open your eyes and look at your partner. When your partner is ready, and also looks up, discuss the experiences you have each just had.

After you have completed this portion of the exercise, leave your erotic refuge and enjoy the pleasures of the everyday, outside world with your partner. Go for a drive, see a movie, order a pizza, or just take a walk around town.

Some time later, return to your erotic refuge and make love. As you do so, do not focus specifically on your earlier, transpersonal experience. Instead, let the insights you have gathered during that experience guide you, on a deep intuitive level, as you focus on providing your partner with as much pleasure as possible.

DAY 18

WITHIN YOU
AND WITHOUT YOU

Today you will take the transpersonal focusing experience a step further by imagining that you have traded places with your partner while *in the midst* of making love.

As you did yesterday, before you begin today's exercise, prepare a plate of fresh fruit and cheese and stock your erotic refuge with the music you enjoy most. Also make sure you have a candle, a candle holder, and some matches. Disconnect or turn off your phone and, in general, arrange to be undisturbed for at least an hour and a half.

Once you have retired to your special room, turn up the thermostat so that you will be completely comfortable in the nude. Then, much like yesterday, take off your clothes and sit on the floor facing your lover. Turn the lights down, light the candle, and place it between you. Make sure you avoid all conversation until the exercise is complete.

Look deeply into your lover's eyes, and, as you do so, inhale and exhale with your lover in synchrony. As you breathe together, imagine that you are sitting in your lover's position looking back at yourself. Then shift your focus back so that you perceive reality as before, from the vantage point of your own body and mind. Continue to synchronize your breathing and shift your focus back and forth until you momentarily feel as though any feelings of separation between you and your lover have dissolved.

Continue to focus for a few minutes, until you sense a deepening feeling of connectedness between you. Now imagine what it feels like to experience reality from within your lover's body. Envision yourself experiencing your lover's sexual feelings. Immerse yourself in these feelings and let them wash through you—through your head and shoulders, down your arms and out your fingers, through your torso, your pelvis, your thighs, your calves, your ankles, and out your toes.

After you have achieved as powerful a sense as possible that you actually exist within your lover's body and mind, hold on to that image while *at the same time* maintaining an equal focus on your own mental and physical existence.

Maintain this focus until both identities seem to inhabit your body at once. Now notice, as you observe your partner's body sitting across from you, how similar it looks in many ways to your own. A woman's breasts, for example, are really more developed versions of a man's. And a man's penis is simply a differently evolved version of a woman's clitoris. Also notice how your bodies differ; look at hair color, hand size, facial hair, skin tone, and anything else that strikes you at all.

> **Sensual Suggestion**—If you and your lover are the same sex, just focus on your differing and similar physical attributes—such as your different body types—and continue with these same instructions.

As you focus, envision your lover's body slowly becoming more like yours, and your body becoming more like your lover's, until you can see the two of you temporarily becoming more androgynous versions of yourselves. As you focus, continue to see yourself from your lover's perspective, as well as from your own.

As you maintain this intensely transpersonal focus, imagine the ways in which your lover's innermost sexual feelings may be similar to yours. (This is a particularly relevant focus for lovers who are members of opposite sexes, because they may not always recognize how their partner's sexual needs and feelings may mirror many of their own.) Imagine how it feels for your partner to experience your body, paying particular attention to those aspects of this experience that you intuitively sense would feel the most exciting and satisfying for your lover.

Hold this image in your mind as you start touching your lover from head to toe. Your lover, of course, should do the same. As you touch each other, remember to strive for whole-body contact—press your chests together, clasp your arms and hands, feel a gentle, then firm, pressure along your thighs. As you touch each other, continue to switch your perspective back and forth from your lover's body and mind to your own. Also continue to maintain the androgynous images you have evoked.

As you continue to make love, envision your bodies literally melding. And finally, imagine yourselves actually trading places. As you and your partner reach orgasm, you should each continue to sustain the idea that this role reversal is complete.

After you have reached orgasm, do not separate. Instead, maintain your whole-body contact and remain sexually attached. Now look at each other and imagine yourselves trading places once more, until your identities have returned to their respective sources. After a few minutes, gently come apart.

When you are ready, we suggest you get dressed in simple, but individualized, clothing and go out for a walk, a cup of coffee, or a drive.

> **Sensual Suggestion**—The day after you and your lover practice this exercise, you should attempt to abandon all preconceived notions of your mutual sexual roles in and out of the bedroom and explore the impact that the exercises of the past two days have had on your understanding of one another and on your overall relationship.

DAY 19

ANDROGYNOUS ACTS

When together, do you and your lover usually take on sexually stereotyped roles? Does one of you usually play a more active role in initiating sexual contact, "leading" your sexual activities like a ballroom dancer leading the dance? Does the other traditionally wait to be seduced before sexually responding to the more active partner? Is one of you more emotionally expressive, the other generally more reserved?

Remember, even partners of the same sex can sometimes find themselves playing traditionally stereotyped sex roles. And even if you and your partner do not assume the stereotypical sex roles, you may find yourselves playing other roles instead. In fact, it's not unusual, especially in today's world, for a woman to earn the greater income while the man spends more time with the kids. There are many female power brokers and many warm, "earth mother" males. Whether you have maintained traditional sex roles or find that, in some aspects of your relationship, at least, these roles have been reversed, clinging to these customary patterns in a rigid, unchanging way may severely limit your potential for erotic pleasure—and for personal fulfillment in many other aspects of your life. Develop the ability to become more flexible in your sexual roles, and you will be freer to express your deepest feelings and desires both within your primary sexual relationship and in society at large.

As we encouraged you to do in the Sensual Suggestion at the end of yesterday's session, begin today's exercise by actively exchanging sex roles with your partner in the course of the day. If your partner usually makes coffee in the morning and takes out the garbage while you make breakfast, try exchanging these jobs. If one of you always pumps the gas and checks the oil and tires while the other does the laundry, this is another opportunity for you both to switch roles.

Before you leave for the day, we would also like you to exchange some articles of clothing. You might, for instance, wear one of your partner's ties or vests, borrow his or her gloves, or trade socks. You might even exchange colognes. As you go through the course of your day, see yourself, in your mind's eye, in your partner's image. When it is comfortable to do so, try to react to situations and events as you feel your partner would. Remember, have fun with this exercise and enjoy the opportunity to break out of the traditional mold.

At some point during the day when you both feel comfortable, you and your partner should enter your erotic refuge. Having relinquished—at least temporarily—your sex roles in the outside world, your goal is to bring this more expansive focus into the overtly sexual aspects of your relationship. If one of you is usually the more passive partner, this partner should take the lead in guiding the exercise and initiating the sexual activities to follow.

Remember, the usually more active partner must not give in to the urge to guide the encounter or comment on the quality of the other's performance, except insofar as this might be necessary to alert the currently active partner to some impending emotional crisis or genuine physical discomfort.

Begin by turning down the lights, removing your clothes, and sitting on the floor directly across from your lover. As you did during yesterday's exercise, light a candle between you, synchronize your breathing, and take some time to practice the transpersonal focusing technique you learned earlier this week. Again, avoid all conversation until the exercise is done.

As you feel a deepening sense of connectedness with your partner, try to experience the sexual feelings you imagine exist within your lover's body. Now, keeping your eyes closed, imagine your partner's body forming around your consciousness and then see it emerging from within your own form.

Finally, you and your partner should make love—again maintaining a role reversal. If one of you is usually in the dominant or more active position, that individual should now take on the more passive or submissive role. You should deliberately imagine yourself having the kinds of sexual feelings you believe your lover usually has during this same sexual act.

By changing places with your partner, you may get a thrilling, even liberating taste of an alternate sexuality. After you and your partner have changed places, you may find yourselves less confined to specific roles from here on in. Remember, personal and sexual freedom emerges only when you play the role of the person you really are. And in all likelihood, the real you may be far more androgynous than you have realized all along.

DAY 20

ANIMAL ATTRACTION

Numerous sexual positions evoke animal forms, from the monkey, the lion, and the bear to the snake and the bird. Just as specific animals arouse in us distinct emotional responses— a lion, for instance, may inspire feelings of agility and aggression —so, too, do these sexual positions have the potential to move us out of a single-pointed, locked-in sexual self-definition toward a whole range of unexplored emotional depths.

To begin exploring this possibility for yourselves, you and your lover should take some time on Day 20 to visit your local zoo or natural history museum. The zoo is preferable, of course, because it gives you an opportunity to closely observe many animals that are moving and alive. If the weather is forbidding, however, or if there is no zoo in your area, you may substitute several exhibits at a local natural history museum. Of course, if you live in a particularly rural area, you may simply be able to go for a drive to observe a bear, a butterfly, a deer, a coyote, or a pasture full of horses or sheep. If, for some reason, none of these alternatives are possible, you may rent or purchase some videotapes of wild animals filmed in their natural surroundings. (As an alternative, you can tape or watch a nature show such as "Wild, Wild World of Animals.")

Whatever your approach, we suggest that you observe as many different types of animals as possible. As you observe the activities of various animals, pay particular attention to the ways in which these creatures move and interact with fellow members of their species. Listen to their sounds, study the expressions that play across their faces and eyes, and notice any special textures or smells. For instance, pay attention to the all-pervasive aroma of the lion house at the zoo, and to the slippery, shiny skin of the seal.

As you study a number of animals, notice if there are any species with which you feel a special personal affinity. Do any animals remind you of yourself, your lover, or the two of you together? Does your lover remind you of a grizzly bear, a wolf, a chipmunk, or a wild boar? Do you remind your lover of an alligator, a sea lion, or a gazelle? Do the two of you make love with the easy gracefulness of two swans floating through a placid pond? Are your lovemaking sessions reminiscent of acrobatic spider monkeys swinging through the trees? Or do the two of you generate the passionate forcefulness of two wild apes in heat?

After you have carried out this first part of today's exercise, and when you feel ready to move to the next phase, return with your lover to your erotic refuge. ("Animal Attraction" should be just as effective whether you wait several hours to seclude yourselves in your erotic refuge or return there immediately.)

As soon as you and your partner enter your erotic refuge, select the animal species you feel you most closely resemble. Your partner, meanwhile, should do the same. *Remember, do not verbally communicate your choices with each other*. As before, make sure the two of you will not be disturbed. Set the thermostat so that the room temperature is as comfortable as possible. And play some appropriate mood music in the background, preferably choosing selections that evoke a sense of wildness and primitive emotion. African tribal music would be among our favorite choices for this exercise, as would many jazz selections—particularly those that emphasize percussion and woodwind instruments.

> **Sensual Suggestion**—As you and your partner begin getting comfortable, take some time to seduce each other before making love. Many couples forget about the pleasures of sexual seduction once they have been together for several months or years. They thereby deprive themselves of the anticipation that can heighten sexual arousal and intensify orgasm.

As you make love with your partner, imagine that the two of you are members of one of the animal species you both observed earlier today. You may take this fantasy as far as it feels comfortable for both of you, providing neither one of you gets injured in the process.

You might, for example, approach your lover with the sexual aggressiveness of an excited bear, or the more gentle and easygoing behavior of a turtle emerging from your shell. Rather than verbalizing your exact intentions to your partner, we suggest that you explore what happens between you when the two of you express your animal fantasies more directly, through your actual sexual behavior.

We must emphasize, however, that it is not necessary for the two of you to pull out all the stops to enhance your sexual experience. You may be extremely subtle in your behavior and still find yourselves surprised by the impact this exercise has on your emotions.

If you feel comfortable doing so, you may even introduce animal sounds into your lovemaking session. The hungry roar of the lion or lioness or the gentle purr of the cat may go a long way toward helping express sexual feelings that have long been pent up.

Remember, however, that not everyone feels comfortable with animal sounds. If you or your partner fit into that category, you might simply communicate through sounds you feel more comfortable with. A gentle and momentary (but decidedly human) ''roar,'' or the excited sound of an orgasmic shift in breathing, may go further for some people than imitating the sounds of a leopard, a tigress, or a chimp. The key is utilizing whatever mode of sexual expression works best for *you*.

At its most subtle and intuitive level, ''Animal Attraction'' should allow you to use nonhuman metaphors to get in touch with vital, inner aspects of your own and your partner's sexuality. Even if the two of you were to feel more comfortable not actually playing out the sexual roles of various animals, identifying with certain animals can deepen your understanding of one another's sexual feelings. It can also bring you into more intimate contact with some long-buried aspects of your own inner nature.

> **Sensual Suggestion**—Sometime after you have finished making love, you might want to sit down with your partner and discuss what "Animal Attraction" has helped you to learn about yourselves.

DAY 21

FIELD OF DREAMS

On Day 21 you will attempt to evoke the presence of your lover in a *lucid* dream. A lucid dream is one in which you are aware of the fact that you are dreaming while in the midst of the dream. (For detailed instructions on lucid dreaming, see our book, *Lucid Dreams in 30 Days: The Creative Sleep Program*. New York: St. Martin's Press, 1989.) Once you have conjured the presence of your lover in a lucid dream, you should be able to act out your most forbidden sexual fantasies and uncover unconscious erotic desires you didn't even know you had.

Today, we would like you and your partner to spend the hours before lunchtime exploring the difference between complete waking consciousness and dream sleep. As you go about your business, we would like you to ask yourselves, every so often, whether you are awake or dreaming. Every half hour or so, stop, look around you, and simply ask yourself, *Is this a dream?*

Let's say you're taking a subway from your apartment to your downtown firm. First study the people around you. Do they have normal, everyday faces? Or does that young mother to your left boast a third eye blinking in the middle of her forehead? What about the colorfully painted billboard to your right? Look at the images displayed on it once, then look again. Are the images different each time you view them, or the same? If they differ from one moment to the next, and you're not looking at some newfangled, high-tech billboard, you must be dreaming.

One of the best ways to check whether or not you're dreaming is to deliberately change some aspect of your immediate surroundings through thought alone. For example, let's say you're seated in a clam bar and a waiter brings you six clams on the half shell. Before you dive in, look at the plate and mentally will the six clams into twelve. If the transformation takes place, you are most certainly in a dream. Continue to ask yourself, *Is this a dream?* throughout the rest of the day. Then answer your question with an appropriate reality check.

Remember, you can usually recognize a dream through the occurrence of anything weirdly inappropriate or bizarre—particularly if you can bring about such occurrences through deliberate thought. For instance, if you are breathing underwater without scuba gear or traversing the vastness of outer space in a jet-propelled body suit, you are probably dreaming.

After lunch, continue testing everyday reality. However, we would like you to add another element to your reality check. Every half hour or so, simply tell yourself, *Tonight I will recognize that I am dreaming while in the midst of a dream.*

> **Sensual Suggestion**—Read through the rest of the "Field of Dreams" exercise two or three times before going on. In that way, you will not have to interrupt your spontaneous sexual encounter to refer to this book.

In the evening, after you and your partner have returned from your daily adventures, share a romantic meal. But remember to keep it light. After all, you don't want to feel so full that you inhibit your sexual activities. We particularly suggest such sensuous foods as mild but tasty gourmet cheeses, chocolate cognac sauce, olives, Belon oysters, or a large bowl of ripe and succulent fruit. A combination of honeydew melon, crenshaw melon, and cantaloupe mixed with sweet strawberries and a splash of Grand Marnier would be ideal. You may also want to share some semidry red wine or fruit juice.

While you and your partner enjoy your sensuous repast, spend the time touching each other and talking about sex. Specifically, we would like you to talk as honestly as possible about what you plan and desire for a session of sexual abandon to follow. For instance, you might say, *I want to lick the inside of your calves, the inside of your thighs, and the inside of your vagina*, or *Let's pretend we're prehistoric cave dwellers before a sacrifice, all worked into a dark, ferocious heat*. Do you desire oral sex? Would you like your partner to wear metal, spikes, and leather? Do you crave musk-scented massage oil heated in the microwave or over a flame and then rubbed over your back? Whatever your fancy, express it verbally, now.

After you've finished eating, take a luxurious bath or shower together, slowly soaping each other all over and touching each other in special, sexual places. Then spend at least two hours massaging each other's bodies with warm, scented oil, touching, hugging and kissing each other, and passionately making love. You might also enhance the atmosphere by playing sexy music, lighting candles, or burning incense.

As you make love, remember to touch each other all over and to make head-to-toe, whole-body contact. Pick out some favorite sexual thing to do, such as slowly stroking your partner into increasingly powerful multiple orgasms, or taking your partner's sexual organs in your mouth and bringing him or her to climax. Then think of something equally exciting for your partner to do to you.

Also take this opportunity to use some of the "objects of desire" you explored in Week Two. Feathers and straws, colorful scarves and beads, a moistened cotton swab, a water atomizer, bottles of natural oil, jars of jelly or gourmet preserves, fake fur mittens, garters, cotton swabs, hand-held mirrors, spiked high-heeled shoes, fine paintbrushes, flowers, and even flashlights can add to your enjoyment now.

Forget about the world outside your erotic refuge, and for now just concentrate on each other. If animal sounds enhance your excitement, make them now. Use transpersonal focusing techniques to merge on as deep an emotional and erotic level as possible. Imagine what it feels like to experience reality from within your lover's body. Envision yourself experiencing your lover's sexual feelings. Immerse yourself in these feelings, and let them wash through you—through your head and shoulders, down your arms and out your fingers, through your torso, your pelvis, your thighs, your calves, your ankles, and out your toes. As you approach orgasm, see your bodies literally melding. Make love until you are both exhausted and ready to fall into an easy sleep.

After you have both climaxed for the last time tonight, do not separate. Instead, maintain your whole body contact and remain as sexually attached as possible. While maintaining this position, look at each other and discuss the mutual lucid dream you will incubate now. Is there a particular fantasy you would like to act out, one that you'd never be comfortable fulfilling in real life, such as including someone else in your lovemaking or dressing up in costumes and playing different roles? Is there a particular place you'd like to make love—the beachfront on Waikiki at midnight, the foothills of the Himalayas, under the blankets on an in-flight plane? Discuss these fantasies openly, and don't be afraid to let your discussions lead into more lovemaking. You may act these fantasies out taking different roles. Just be sure to establish some sort of focus for your mutual lucid dream scenario. Continue making love until you both fall asleep.

As you fall asleep in each other's arms, focus on your mutual lucid dream scenario and tell yourselves that you will recognize you are dreaming while in the midst of your dreams. As you drift off to sleep, you might even repeat the phrase: *Tonight I will recognize that I am dreaming while in the midst of a dream.*

If all goes well, reality checks conducted *while you are dreaming* will tip you off to the fact that you are, in fact, in a dream. Once you realize you are in a dream, the lucid dream state should kick in.

For many people, however, a further technique, practiced in the early-morning hours, will ease the way to lucid dream consciousness. During the early morning hours, you are likely to awaken spontaneously from a nonlucid dream. When you do, lie quietly in bed without moving or opening your eyes and think about the dream you've just had. Review the dream in your mind in as much detail as possible, absorbing the emotional impact of the setting, characters, plot, and overall aesthetic imagery. (Remember, it does not matter whether or not your partner was in this dream. Once you find yourself in a lucid dream, you should be able to seek out your partner in the dream landscape.) Review the dream several times in your thoughts until you've more or less committed it to conscious memory.

Then review the dream again, this time adding one element that was clearly missing before: As you replay the dream in your thoughts, approach it as if you, the dreamer, are conscious of the dream as it is happening. Repeat the phrase, *I will recognize a dream when I am dreaming* and allow yourself to drift off to sleep.

If you follow these instructions, you will probably find yourself falling backward from your nearly conscious state into the realm of sleep and dreams. You may possibly find yourself replaying the dream you just left, or generating a whole new dream that may or may not include elements of your previous dream. In either case, you may soon find yourself in the midst of a full-blown lucid dream. Of course, if you find yourself generating a lucid dream with this technique, you should still conduct a reality check just to make sure.

Once you find yourself in the midst of a lucid dream, look around the dream landscape for your partner. If you do not see your partner, walk around until you find him—or simply will her into existence.

Once you have found your partner, focus on fulfilling your sexual fantasy together in your lucid dream. As the dream proceeds, you should find you can even invoke the presence of scintillating dream scenery and props. As you carry out your intentions, you may find yourself in the midst of some of the most exciting, unbridled sex of your life.

> *Sensual Suggestion*—Because some people may find it difficult to experience a full-blown lucid dream or a full-scale dream sex encounter the very first time, it may be helpful to practice the "Field of Dreams" techniques for several nights running. Practicing this approach on a regular basis, moreover, may help you explore your sexual fantasies in your dreams.

> *Sensual Suggestion*—If you find yourself moving toward waking consciousness while practicing this exercise, just continue to act out your fantasy in your semiconscious imagination.

> *Sensual Suggestion*—When you wake up in the morning, lie completely still and keep your eyes closed. Let the details of all your lucid and nonlucid dreams float back to you. Keep your eyes closed until you have recalled as many details as possible, then share your dream experience with your partner. The two of you may also consider acting out your sexual and nonsexual dreams together, at least in part, in waking reality.

After practicing this exercise and reviewing your dream experiences together, you and your partner should share some low-key, nonsexual activity—like playing Scrabble or going for a walk in the park—to maintain a sense of balance and reaffirm your waking connection. Besides, it's time to celebrate. You have just completed Week Three of the Erotic Fulfillment Program!

WEEK THREE INTUITIVE SEX

DAY 15 FORTRESS OF SOLITUDE	**DAY 16** MIRRORING		**DAY 17** TRANS- PERSONAL FOCUSING	
Spend at least a couple of hours away from your lover.	Retire to your erotic refuge with your part- ner.	Ultimately, both you and your partner should act out the fantasy to- gether, in a sort of slow motion dance.	Prepare a plate of fresh fruit and cheese and stock your erotic refuge with the music you most en- joy.	
Enjoy the lux- ury of being alone.	Remove your clothes and sit across from each other.			
While by your- self, notice the overall feeling of your body.	Each of you, in turn, should consider and act out—with- out talking—a desired sexual fantasy.	Abandon the pantomime and guide your lover's hand to demonstrate the ways that you like to be touched.	Take off your clothes and sit on the floor facing your partner.	
Focus on your innermost sex- ual and emo- tional feelings toward your lover.			Turn the lights down, light a candle, and place it be- tween you.	
Return home and enter your erotic refuge by yourself.	After one of you has done a pantomime of this fantasy, the other should mirror that pantomime as closely as possible.	Remove your hand and allow your lover to touch you in- dependently. Switch roles.	Breathe in syn- chrony with your partner.	
Enter a state of alert relaxa- tion.			Look into your lover's eyes, and as you do so, imagine that you are perceiving the world from within his or her body.	
Imagine mak- ing love with your partner.	If the mirror- ing is not ac- curate, the first person can act out the desired fantasy again.			

DAY 18
WITHIN YOU
AND WITHOUT
YOU

Maintain this focus until all feelings of separation between you have dissolved.

Close your eyes and lower your heads. Allow your breathing to return to normal and reassimilate your sense of self.

Discuss your mutual experiences.

Leave your erotic refuge to enjoy the pleasures of the everyday world.

Return to your erotic refuge and make love.

Prepare a plate of fresh fruit and cheese and stock your erotic refuge with the music you most enjoy.

Take off your clothes and sit on the floor facing your partner.

Turn the lights down, light a candle and place it between you.

Breathe in synchrony with your partner.

Look into your lover's eyes, and as you do so, imagine that you are perceiving the world from within his or her body. At the same time, continue to view the world from your own perspective.

Maintain this focus until all feelings of separation between you have dissolved.

Notice how similar your partner's body is to your own.

Envision your two bodies becoming more and more alike.

Imagine ways in which your lover's innermost sexual feelings may be similar to your own.

Start to gently touch your lover from head to toe, and as you do so, envision how it feels for your partner to experience your body.

Imagine trading places.

Experience orgasm.

Maintain whole-body contact.

Slowly separate and resume your everyday perspective.

DAY 19
ANDROGYNOUS
ACTS

DAY 20
ANIMAL
ATTRACTION

Start the day by actively exchanging roles with your partner.

Swap some articles of clothing.

Enter your erotic refuge with your partner.

Take off your clothes and sit on the floor facing your partner.

Turn the lights down, light a candle, and place it between you.

Breathe in synchrony with your partner.

Look into your lover's eyes, and as you do so, imagine that you are perceiving the world from within his or her body. At the same time, continue to view the world from your own perspective.

Maintain this focus until all feelings of separation between you have dissolved.

Make love. If one partner is normally more active, that partner should play a less active role now. If one partner is normally less active, that partner should play a more active role now.

Visit your local zoo or natural history museum.

Observe the animals.

Return to your erotic refuge with your partner.

Select the animal species you feel you most closely resemble. Remember: Do not verbally communicate your choice to your partner.

Play mood music that evokes a sense of wildness and primitive emotion.

Make love. As you do, imagine that you are both members of the animal species you selected earlier. Remember, you and your partner may each envision a different species.

Sometime later sit down with your partner and discuss what this exercise has taught you.

DAY 21
FIELD OF
DREAMS

From time to time as you go about your day, stop and ask yourself whether you are dreaming.

Tell yourself that tonight, while in the midst of a dream, you will recognize that you are dreaming.

Share a light but romantic meal with your partner.

While you eat, touch each other and talk about sex.

Take a bath or shower together.

Make passionate love.

Take some time to discuss the details of the dream you hope to share.

As you fall asleep, focus on your mutual lucid dream scenario.

As you fall asleep, tell yourself, *Tonight I will recognize I am dreaming while in the midst of a dream.*

If you wake up in the middle of the night, recall your last dream in as much detail as possible. While reviewing the dream, approach it as if you, the dreamer, are conscious of the dream as it is happening. Then repeat the phrase *I will recognize a dream when I am dreaming*, and fall back to sleep.

Once you find yourself in the midst of a lucid dream, look around the dream landscape for your partner.

Fulfill your sexual fantasies in your dream.

After you wake up, discuss your dreams with your partner.

Share some low-key, non-sexual activity with your partner.

WEEK FOUR

COSMIC CONNECTIONS

WEEK FOUR

•

C O S M I C
C O N N E C T I O N S

*Y*ou will spend the rest of the Erotic Fulfillment Program exploring the mystical dimensions of sex. As you will discover in the course of Week Four, sexual intimacy and orgasm can lead you directly to a sense of timelessness, a sense of connectedness with the Earth and the universe, a deeper sense of meaning, and feelings of reverie and bliss.

As in Week Three, you will begin by spending a little time on your own enjoying the sexually recuperative influence of a little abstinence. You will also begin integrating the transpersonal focusing experiences of the past week by taking your relationship back in time—to the point at which you and your lover first got together and established your sexual connection.

In your journey toward generating a mystical state of mind, you will explore the real-life fantasy of outdoor sex, which can help you and your lover feel closer to each other and the natural world. You will also explore the expansive potential of your inner sexuality by pursuing the powerful altered states of consciousness that can emerge through orgasm. You will learn how to follow these altered states to a mystical sense of union with the universe; to the otherworldly perception that your mind and body exist in separate planes; and to a sense of connection to the far future and distant past. In the end, your sexual energy may feel like a force potent enough to drive all forms of matter, from the tiniest whirling atoms to the elegant dancing galaxies curving out from the center of the universe.

As in Week Three, the Week Four exercises are potentially powerful and intense. Therefore, we advise you to skip the last three exercises of this week if you have strong unresolved conflicts about death, if you have serious psychiatric or psychological problems (unless you choose to consult with your therapist while undertaking these exercises), or if you are under the influence of mind-altering drugs.

That said, just open your mind, your heart—and your innermost sexuality—to the Week Four exercises. You and your lover should reap great sexual pleasure from this erotic journey through the unexplored boundaries of space and time.

DAY 22

FIRST DATE

Today's two-part exercise, which follows an intense week of transpersonal sex, calls for complete sexual abstinence. During the first part of this exercise, you should find yourself regaining your personal equilibrium and reaffirming the nonsexual aspects of the friendship you share with your partner. During the second part of this exercise, you should recapture the romantic impulse that first drew you and your lover together.

As we suggested near the end of the instructions for Day 21, spend this morning engaged in some low-key, nonsexual activity with your partner. Whether you decide to play Monopoly or simply share a bowl of cereal before you head off to your individual jobs, use this time to reaffirm your friendship with each other.

Once you and your lover part, however, you should make an effort to stay away from each other until this evening. Spend the day devoting yourself to the mundane details of your life. If today is a regular working day for you, get involved with your tasks at the office, the lab, the factory, or out in the field. If you have today off, go shopping for some clothes you have needed, take a trip to the bookstore, or catch up on some household chores.

In the early evening, after you have left work or completed some personal housekeeping, get ready to reacquaint yourself with your lover. You will do so by going on a fantasy date, in which you'll both pretend the two of you are meeting again for the very first time.

Get ready for your date by dressing up in a fashion that you believe will be as attractive as possible for your partner. This does not necessarily mean that you need to wear a leather miniskirt or jeans so tight they physically prevent you from becoming sexually aroused. It means simply that you should look your absolute best, with a particular emphasis on what you know will most please your lover. For some this might mean renting a tuxedo, for others it could just as well mean digging out an old pair of overalls and a plaid, flannel shirt.

Greet your "date" at the front door, or meet at a restaurant. Bring flowers, candy, or some other gift suitable for a special man or woman with whom you are just getting acquainted. If possible, you might even consider returning to the same place you spent your very first date.

Allow yourselves to recapture the mood of that very first experience. What were you thinking about when you first met this person? What did you like about him or her, and what really drew the two of you together?

Since you and your partner are acting out the fantasy of just having met, take this opportunity to learn as much as you can about one another. If you listen carefully, you are sure to learn something you really never have heard before. Clearly, this is not the time to discuss concerns about bills, children, getting the car repaired, taking the cat to the vet, or anything else that might crop up in the course of a long-term relationship.

As you sit enjoying dinner with your "date," allow your thoughts to wander to the kind of sexual fantasies you must have been having about him or her on that very first night. Without losing the natural subtlety of the moment, mentally undress your companion. Fantasize about what he or she must really look like under all of those clothes, right here and right now. What do you imagine it might be like to make love with this person?

Complete your date with a good-night kiss, but nothing more overtly sexual. Allow yourself to fully experience any pangs of sexual frustration this may arouse in you. But do not follow through on these feelings by bringing yourself to orgasm.

Remember, since you and your "date" have just met, you should also consider sleeping apart this evening, as you would with anyone you've just met. If you do sleep together, we suggest you sleep in your clothes and, at least for tonight, establish some personal space.

As you drift off to sleep, focus your thoughts entirely on this romantic day or evening. Fantasize about what it might be like one day to make love with the man or woman you have just gotten to know on your date.

> **Sensual Suggestion**—When you wake up in the morning, greet your lover with warmth—a hug, a kind word, a hot cup of coffee. The two of you may now feel entirely free to openly discuss your feelings about yesterday's exercise.

DAY 23

LAST COMMUNION

Today you and your partner will once more conduct a dialogue. As in the "First Communion" exercise of Week Two, your goal will be to enhance the intuitive skills that can take you and your lover to a higher, more intimate sexual plane. As before, you will communicate with your partner in an open, totally honest way. By sharing your feelings about the Erotic Fulfillment Program and your place in the broader world, you will enhance your mutual intimacy and your sexual rapport.

> **Sensual Suggestion**—If, as we suggested during Week Two, you and your partner have participated in communion every week at a regular time, simply integrate the suggestions for this "Last Communion" into your established format. However, if you have not held communion since Week Two, please follow the directions here as closely as possible.

To hold your last communion, retire to your erotic refuge with your partner at a time when you feel you will have at least an hour without being disturbed. Then change into loose, flowing clothes and share some fresh fruit, cheese, or wine. Before you begin your actual talk, we would like you to remember to tell the truth, to listen carefully to your partner, and to be supportive of what he or she says, no matter what that might be. Do not make your lover feel guilty for any thoughts or feelings, and try to avoid feelings of guilt yourself. As you speak, look into your partner's eyes.

Address the issues below, in order. After you have both given your answers, each should try to do his or her best to respond to what the other has said. Remember, this is not the time to be judgmental. No matter what your partner tells you, be as loving and accepting as you can.

- Do you feel that you and your partner know each other better than you did before? If so, how has your increased knowledge influenced your sexual and overall relationship?

- Are there any sexual requests you have not yet discussed with each other? If so, do so now. And be as explicit as possible.

- Describe the precise way that you perceive your partner while making love. Be as explicit as possible.

- If you have any sexual fantasies you feel are too extreme to actually act on, you may (if you want) discuss these with your partner now.

Sensual Suggestion—After you have held your last communion, take some time to gently make love.

DAY 24

STONE SONGS

Today you will enjoy an erotic interlude with your lover in some secluded, natural setting. The spot you choose should be safe and, of course, fairly immune to the possibility of outside intrusion. In the best of all possible worlds, you would carry out this exercise on private land owned by you or a friend. You might also arrange to seclude yourselves on the deck of a boat anchored in the ocean, in a tent pitched in your backyard, or inside a comfortable cave far away from the prying eyes of civilization. If the weather is cold or treacherous in your part of the universe, you might rent a room or cabin at a particularly rustic, out-of-the-way motel or inn.

If you are feeling truly adventurous and are fortunate enough to find some safe and suitable spot, you may even wish to make love right on the beach, alongside a river, or at the edge of a lake in the forest. After all, the sound of moving water, be it crashing waves or a bubbling stream, can create an unparalleled, outwardly calming yet inwardly stirring sexual mood. Perhaps the presence of water arouses some unconscious, primordial aspect of human awareness, or perhaps the aquatic rhythms simply distract us from our outside concerns.

Begin by exploring your immediate surroundings on foot with your lover. Imagine yourselves existing in a world apart from mainstream society—perhaps you are two primitive humans taking time away from your tribe to enjoy a long-anticipated romantic encounter; perhaps you are the last remaining human survivors following some natural or manmade global disaster. Whatever fantasy you select, it should encourage the two of you to experience mystical communion not only with one another, but with the elements of nature as well.

When you and your lover have completed your walk, get comfortable and retire to your chosen spot. Open yourself up to your immediate setting and let it influence the style you use to make love. You might, for example, slowly undress each other and move very gently into the experience. Or, you might give in to the immediate passions of spontaneous sexual abandon and make love with each other while barely removing your clothes.

As you make love, pay special attention to the smells, sounds, and feelings of your natural surroundings. Contrast these with the familiar smells, sounds, and feelings of your lover. For instance, contrast the cool ocean breeze with your lover's warm, solid body. Contrast the scent of the salt air with that of your lover's hair. Notice the smells of the surrounding air, grass, and plants, and contrast these with the aroma of your lover's skin. Listen to your lover's breathing, and contrast this with the background sounds of birds, katydids, or whistling winds. Allow these rich, sensory impressions to permeate your entire lovemaking experience.

After you and your partner have finished making love, go for another short walk and, once again, experience a feeling of mystical connectedness with one another and with nature.

DAY 25

EARTHLY DELIGHTS

Begin the exercise for Day 25 by returning with your lover to your erotic refuge and making love in whatever manner you've discovered is most pleasurable for you both. We suggest that you allow your lovemaking activities to gradually emerge by first engaging in sexual foreplay incorporating various techniques gleaned to this point from the Erotic Fulfillment Program. You might, for example, first harmonize your breathing with that of your lover's.

You might also stimulate one another with biting and scratching just as you did during Day 11. Feel free to massage each other, to use any erotic objects that enhance your mutual arousal, and to practice transpersonal sex through techniques explored in "Within You and Without You," "Animal Attraction," and "Androgynous Acts." It is especially important that you follow your intuitive sense of what sexual activities you feel your lover will most enjoy at this time.

Then, while you and your partner are in the midst of making love, imagine—as you did during Week One—that your bodies are windows through which you may each envision a variety of distant natural environments. Unlike the Week One exercise, however, in which the scenes you envisioned were more or less independent of your lover's window images, on this occasion you should deliberately complement one another's inner visions and emotions. The most natural way for you both to accomplish this is for one to take an active, and the other a passive, role. (You should then reverse these roles in another session later today or during some future lovemaking experience.)

When you are the active partner, imagine such lively inner scenery as raging forest fires, violent earthquakes, erupting volcanoes overflowing with molten lava, and gray granite mountains being thrust up from the innermost depths of the Earth. Envision these scenes filling your entire body, influencing not only your passing thoughts, but the very manner in which you think about and momentarily experience your own existence and your sexual relationship with your lover.

When you are the passive partner, envision such receptive imagery as the placid surface of a mountain lake, valleys filled with colorful wildflowers, the summer sun beating on golden sand dunes in the desert, and endless fields of freshly fallen snow. You should also imagine these scenes completely filling your entire body, influencing your thoughts and feelings about yourself and the way in which you sexually relate to your lover.

In yet another variation of this exercise, you may both assume active roles and, thus, both generate active inner scenery. You will find that your sex may be particularly scintillating when you both envision running stallions, exploding volcanoes, and bolts of lightning inside your bodies as you make love. When you are both cast in the active role at once, we suggest that you take some time to envision energetic natural scenery in your partner's body as well as your own. By shifting your focus back and forth, from your inner geography to your partner's, you may heighten your level of arousal and render the inner sexual bond with your partner especially strong.

It is not necessary, or even desirable, for you to discuss your inner scenery with your partner while in the midst of making love. It is perfectly appropriate, however, for you both to discuss your experiences after the most intense aspects of this particular lovemaking session have passed, while you are still lying in bed together.

The experience of afterplay is equally as important as foreplay in the evolution of a fulfilling sexual relationship. After reaching climax, therefore, you should continue to remain in close physical union with your lover for some time. Caress each other, play, talk, and laugh. Use this time to complete the experience of intuitive sex with love.

DAY 26

ALTERED STATE ORGASM

Up until now, you and your partner have practiced a variety of consciousness-expanding techniques before and during the lovemaking act. On Day 26, you will carry this expansive focus into the realm of the orgasm and beyond. In fact, the orgasmic state, as you no doubt already realize, can be a consciousness-expanding experience all its own. Orgasm not only allows you to experience a deep sense of mystical communion with your sexual partner, it also often creates a momentary sense of distance and objectivity toward the mundane world around you.

Just as orgasm deepens your sense of connection to your lover, it can also lead to a deeper sense of connectedness with the greater cosmos. Connecting with the universe through orgasm can lead to profound states of heightened sensitivity and awareness that are at least as powerful as those that may be induced through meditation, though some might say that experiencing orgasm is a kind of meditation all its own.

Incidentally, we do not share the perspective of those who recommend permanent sexual abstinence as a method for achieving higher consciousness. In our experience, becoming a more fulfilled human being entails embracing—rather than denying—our normal sexuality as an essential aspect of our overall human nature. It is virtually impossible to achieve a sense of inner wholeness while denying the most basic aspects of oneself.

By now, we will assume that you and your sexual partner have your own ideas and preferences with regard to how you most prefer making love. We will pick up today's exercise, therefore, at the point at which you find yourself on the verge of orgasm.

Sensual Suggestion—It goes without saying that you must read the rest of the instructions for Day 26 before you proceed.

Sensual Suggestion—Do not attempt to carry out this exercise if you have strong unresolved conflicts about death. We also strongly advise against this exercise if you have serious psychiatric or psychological problems, or if you are under the influence of mind-altering drugs.

Just before you experience orgasm, allow your thoughts to move back and forth through time and space. In one moment, feel yourself in the here and now, experiencing the appearance, sounds, feelings, smells, tastes, and movements of your lover's body at every sensual level. Notice the feelings and images that surround you in your immediate environment, and the quickly changing—continuously heightening—feelings of sexual arousal within your body. In the next moment, allow your thoughts to drift into images of you and your lover in the past. Envision the time you first got together. Recall the significant moments in the course of your relationship. And see, in your mind's eye, the erotic pleasure you have experienced during the past three and a half weeks of the Erotic Fulfillment Program.

Then immediately allow your thoughts to shift back, once again, to the present, experiencing the closeness of your lover and the timeless impact of this particular moment. Feel the connection between this orgasm and all other orgasms you've ever experienced with your lover. Imagine this experience as an underlying thread or theme running continuously through your relationship.

Now shift your focus of attention toward the greater cosmos. Notice how it feels to be a human being with a body, and focus on your personal existence in the universe. Then envision the existence you share with your partner in this transitory moment in time and space. Experience the impact of orgasm as an affirmation of your unique personal existence and the existence you share with your partner in the cosmos at large.

After you and your partner have both reached orgasm, stay physically attached and maintain whole-body contact. As you do so, envision the immediate environment disappearing from all around you. Still intertwined with your partner, see yourselves floating out in space at the center of the universe. Imagine that you and your lover are two particles floating in harmony with all other particles in the universe, moving in response to the rhythms of electrons and protons, neutrons and quarks. Now imagine that the two of you are really one particle, two eternally connected aspects of one experience, floating in the infinite void of space.

Finally, allow your thoughts to shift back to the here and now, to the real and profound impact of being with your lover in this exact moment. Recall those aspects of your everyday life—your home, family, sense of ordinary reality—that make you feel most intimately connected with who you really are.

Sensual Suggestion—If you and your lover are able to experience mutual orgasms, this exercise may be even more profound for both of you and may lead to subjectively shared consciousness-expanding experiences. It is not, however, in any way essential that you experience mutual orgasms in order to explore the potentially powerful impact of this exercise.

DAY 27

A SPACE ODYSSEY

On Day 27, you will carry the consciousness-expanding dimensions of orgasm one step further—into the unique realm of the out-of-body experience, or OBE. As we have discussed in detail in our previous volume, *Have an Out-of-Body Experience in 30 Days: The Free Flight Program* (New York: St. Martin's Press, 1989), OBEs are simply altered states of consciousness in which you feel a subjective sense of distance and separation from your body. One of the most effective methods for inducing the OBE can be practiced in the aftermath of orgasm.

Sensual Suggestion—By all means, read the instructions for Day 27 through to the end before you begin.

As in yesterday's exercise, pick up today's session just before you and your lover reach orgasm. As before, allow your thoughts to drift back and forth in time and space, focusing both on your immediate emotions and sensations, and on images of you and your lover at different points throughout your relationship.

Now close your eyes and while you are on the verge—or in the midst—of orgasm, imagine you and your lover floating up, up, up. See yourselves as twin points of consciousness floating in tandem over your bodies below. Look down and, in your mind's eye, see your bodies making love. Allow yourself to experience as much distance from the physical reality "below" you as is comfortably possible.

Finally, shift your focus of attention toward the greater cosmos. See yourself and your lover floating in tandem in the endless vacuum of space. Look down and, in your mind's eye, see your two bodies making love back on Earth. Now you may experience an even greater sense of distance from physical reality than you did before.

As your bodies reach orgasm, your minds should achieve a deep sense of union with each other and with the cosmos at large.

Conclude this experience by focusing once more on your own and your lover's body, and on familiar aspects of ordinary reality that make you feel intimately connected with your own everyday existence. Open your eyes and once again feel a solid connection to the here and now—but remember to savor the lingering sensations and images associated with your recent orgasm and OBE.

> **Sensual Suggestion**—You and your lover may wish to choose an erotic and romantic place to mentally "visit" while in the midst of your mutual OBEs. Instead of envisioning the space above your bed or the greater cosmos, simply picture the Caribbean, the Left Bank of Paris, or the Caspian Sea. Then focus on the place you've chosen while joined in a moment of orgasmic passion. Maintain your mental images while focusing on your emotional and sexual feelings for as long as is comfortably possible. You can even imagine yourselves communicating with one another in your thoughts—without talking—during this experience. For a particularly interesting variation, you might focus on inducing a mutual out-of-body experience without selecting a predetermined "destination." Then compare notes later on.

> **Sensual Suggestion**—If you don't share an OBE with your lover the first time you practice this exercise, do not be concerned or put pressure on yourself or your partner. Instead, simply repeat this exercise on a regular basis and allow the desired experience to evolve over time.

> **Sensual Suggestion**—Avoid this exercise if you have serious unresolved conflicts about death, or if you have serious psychological problems. In such a case, we recommend checking with your therapist before attempting the "Space Odyssey" technique. We also suggest that you avoid this exercise if you are under the influence of any mind-altering drugs.

DAY 28

THE OUTER LIMITS

On Day 28, you will carry the overall focus of the past two days into an expanding sense of timelessness and inner connectedness with all of humanity and the universe as a whole. Begin today's exercise the moment you enter your erotic refuge with your lover. The room should be lit exclusively by candlelight or through the soft glow of a red or pink bulb. There should also be gentle, expansive music playing in the background. We suggest such composers as Vivaldi, Brahms, or Strauss.

As you initially make sexual contact, look into your lover's eyes and ask, in your thoughts, *Where have I known you before?* As you focus on this question, imagine your lover's face and body changing dimensions, momentarily becoming many different faces and bodies from many different times and places throughout human history. Imagine that your face and body are also shifting dimensions from moment to moment; envision your lover observing these changes as they occur. You may use this initial phase of the exercise to imagine that you and your lover are experiencing an altered form of existence, or you may focus on your evolutionary connection to other human beings throughout the course of history—including the present time. Eventually, see your form and your lover's form shift back to the way you really are.

Whatever fantasy you entertain, imagine that the two of you as a sexual couple now are only a current expression of an ongoing experience of sexual connectedness that you have in common with every other human couple that has ever been alive on this planet— and especially with your own immediate spiritual and/or evolutionary ancestors. Allow this experience to give you a sense of connectedness with the broader spectrum of humanity throughout all time. Then expand your focus outward, to include such nonhuman couples as animals, birds, insects, and flowers. Imagine your sexual union with your lover as only one expression of a broader and more timeless principle of universal sexual connectedness.

Then focus, once again, on the here and now, and continue making increasingly intimate sexual contact with your lover. As you do so, allow your thoughts to drift back and forth in time and space, focusing on your immediate emotions and sensations, on images of you both at various points throughout your relationship, and on broader and more expansive images of sexual connectedness throughout all space and time.

Say to yourself, in your thoughts, *We are sharing this sexual connection throughout all space and time.* Without becoming overly analytical in this focus, make love with your partner, moving more and more closely toward the height of orgasm. As you near the moment of sexual climax, close your eyes and turn your thoughts toward the greater cosmos, imagining your immediate surroundings dissolving into the universe as a whole.

Now imagine that you and your partner, still making love, are floating together at the center of the universe, and that you have always been there and will always be there. Imagine that the rhythm of this sexual experience is the underlying rhythm of the entire cosmos. Imagine that the expansion and contraction of your love-making drives all expansion and contraction in the universe throughout space and time.

Maintain this focus for a minute or two after you and your partner have experienced orgasm, then gradually let the experience go. Feel yourself safe and secure, and consider your body from the same perspective you had before. Open your eyes and tell yourself that the rhythms of the universe, which you have just experienced, will continue to express themselves through the deep inner rhythms of your body every time you make love. Then once again feel a solid connection to the here and now—but remember to savor the lingering sensations and images associated with your recent journey beyond.

Sensual Suggestion—Once again, if you don't achieve the desired state the first time you practice this exercise, don't be concerned or put pressure on yourself or your partner. Just repeat the exercise whenever it feels right for both of you, and allow the experience to evolve over time.

Sensual Suggestion—Again, do not attempt to carry out this exercise if you have strong unresolved conflicts about death. We also strongly

advise against this exercise if you have serious psychiatric or psychological problems, or if you are under the influence of mind-altering
drugs.

Congratulations! You have just completed Week Four of the
Erotic Fulfillment Program.

WEEK FOUR   COSMIC CONNECTIONS

DAY 22 FIRST DATE		DAY 23 LAST COMMUNION	DAY 24 STONE SONGS	
Engage in some low-key, nonsexual activity with your partner. Separate from your partner, and spend the rest of the day apart. Toward the evening, go home and get ready for a fantasy date with your partner. Greet your date in a romantic fashion. Go to a restaurant, coffee shop, amusement park, or wherever else you wish, and recapture the mood of your original meeting weeks, months, or years before.	Learn as much as you can about each other. Entertain the same sexual fantasies you had about your partner upon first meeting. Complete your date with a good-night kiss. Sleep apart, or, if you prefer, sleep together but remain dressed.	Retire to your erotic refuge with your partner. Change into loose, flowing clothes and share some fresh fruit, cheese, or wine. Remember to tell the truth, listen carefully and be supportive. Address the issues presented in the text for Day 23, one by one. If you so desire, gently make love.	Visit a secluded natural setting. Explore the surroundings on foot. Imagine yourselves existing apart from mainstream society. Retire to your chosen, secluded spot. Open yourselves up to your immediate surroundings and let the ambience permeate your mood as you make love. After you have finished making love, go for a walk and allow yourselves to experience a sense of mystical connectedness with each other and your environment.	

DAY 25
EARTHLY
DELIGHTS

DAY 26
ALTERED STATE
ORGASM

Retire to your erotic refuge with your partner and make love.

In the midst of your lovemaking, imagine that your bodies are windows through which you may envision a variety of distant natural environments.

One of you may take an active sexual role and imagine energetic images such as volcanoes and rolling oceans. The other may take a less active role and imagine placid images such as trickling streams or fields of grass.

Shift your focus back and forth from your own inner geography to your partner's.

Exchange roles.

Then, if you like, you may both take on active sexual roles—and generate active inner images.

After you have finished making love, remain in close physical union.

Discuss your experiences.

Make love in the way you and your partner enjoy most.

Just before you experience orgasm, allow your thoughts to move back and forth through space and time.

Shift your thoughts back to the present.

Shift your focus of attention out toward the greater cosmos.

Envision the existence you share with your partner at this particular moment in time and space as you reach orgasm.

After climax, stay as physically connected as possible.

See yourself and your partner floating out in space at the center of the universe.

Shift your thoughts back to the here and now.

DAY 27
A SPACE
ODYSSEY

DAY 28
THE OTHER
LIMITS

Make love in the way you and your partner enjoy most.

Just before you experience orgasm, allow your thoughts to move back and forth through space and time.

While in the midst of orgasm, imagine you and your lover floating up.

See yourselves as twin points of consciousness floating in tandem over your bodies.

Look down and, in your mind's eye, see yourselves making love.

Shift your focus of attention toward the greater cosmos.

See yourself and your lover floating in space.

Look down again, and again see your bodies making love.

As your bodies reach orgasm, feel your minds unite with each other and with the universe at large.

Focus once more on your body, your lover's body, and ordinary reality.

Enter your erotic refuge with your lover.

Light the room exclusively with candles or with a red or pink bulb.

Play gentle, expansive music.

See many different faces and bodies from many times and places reflected in your partner's form.

Imagine your face going through similar shifts.

See your lover's form and your own as they really are.

Feel a sense of connectedness to all of humanity throughout time.

Make love.

As you reach orgasm, imagine your immediate surroundings dissolving into the greater universe.

Imagine you and your partner floating together at the center of the universe. Imagine that your sexual energy fuels the entire universe.

Look around and feel a solid connection to the here and now.

DAYS 29 AND 30

THE LOST WEEKEND

The Erotic Fulfillment Program has taught you and your lover the basic skills for developing a more expansive, intuitive, and fulfilling sexual relationship. You may have found some of the exercises we've presented more suited to your sexual preferences and background than others. This is normal and should be expected, since your sexuality is ultimately a deeply personal matter and different people will respond to the various exercises in different ways. Now that you've had an opportunity to explore all the exercises, we suggest you continue refining the Inner Sex techniques that have worked best for you. We encourage you to continue developing your innermost sexuality. Eventually, you may personalize our techniques to such a degree that, in effect, you will have developed an Erotic Fulfillment Program of your own.

We recommend that you spend Days 29 and 30 on an erotic retreat, taking time together away from the usual pressures of your daily lives and the more structured sexual experiences of the past four weeks. If you can fit this into your budget and schedule, it would be best for the two of you to go away on Days 29 and 30— or as soon as possible—to some secret romantic spot. A quaint motel on the outskirts of your city, a two-day visit to the shore, or a trip to a cabin in the woods would serve the purpose well.

While on your lost weekend, avoid associating with other people unless it is absolutely necessary. This is not the time to catch that great Italian film at the local theater or try that new Cajun restaurant. (You can always pack some extra videos along with wine and cheese and other gourmet items in your suitcase.)

If it is impossible for you to get away, you can have a lost weekend at home. Just lock your front door, unplug the phone, and spend the time making sensuous meals, watching old movies, and making wild, passionate love. If you do decide to stay home, however, remember that this is not a weekend for catching up on paperwork or inviting the neighbors in for lunch. The point is to quietly get "lost" this weekend and spend the time enjoying one another on any level you choose without outside interruptions.

To truly turn this weekend's erotic retreat into a personal Shangri-

La, we suggest that you and your partner spend at least part of your time imagining yourselves immersed in some ancient or future society, one that regularly practices the sexual rites you have rehearsed during the past four weeks. You can also invent for your society some sexual practices you have thus far experienced only in your mind, when alone.

At first, you and your partner might invent separate, secret worlds. As you create your inner sexual society, see every last detail, from the leather thongs, lush fur togas, and amethyst studs worn by the inhabitants, for instance, to the vast crystal chambers where they live and sleep. Then imagine the sex—soft and spontaneous, under a torrent of sunlight, for instance, or impassioned, even rough, atop the wet clay mounds that serve as beds.

After you have each envisioned a private erotic world, share your creations with each other. Then spend the next few hours reenacting the scenarios, wrapping yourselves in an emotional envelope where the two secret societies have mystically merged.

At some point after you have existed in this joint erotic universe for a while, we suggest that you use "Dream Weaving" and "Field of Dreams" techniques to incubate shared or lucid dreams in which you meet—and make love—in your Shangri-La while you sleep. The dream sex you experience should be especially rich and intense.

Feel free to enter and leave your secret society at will throughout the duration of your lost weekend. When not "in" your fantasy society, spend your time making love, making meals, listening to music, and talking. Use any Inner Sex technique you find fulfilling: Softly scratch and bite each other, use feathers and straws, assume the identity of animals, swap identities during orgasm, or induce the sensation that you and your lover are two points of consciousness floating in space. Most of all, just take time out of the rush of your lives to enjoy one another and remember what brought you together in the first place. That is often the surest route of all to erotic fulfillment.

We wish you all the best in the future of your relationship, and extend our warmest wishes and congratulations. You've just graduated from the Erotic Fulfillment Program!

A SPECIAL NOTE TO THE PHYSICALLY DISABLED

*F*or the sake of simplicity, the instructions for many of the exercises in the Erotic Fulfillment Program appear to assume certain basic physical capabilities. We sincerely hope, however, that the Erotic Fulfillment Program will attract a diverse readership, including many individuals who may have a wide variety of physical disabilities and sexual proclivities and tastes. In fact, there is absolutely no reason why the techniques presented in the Erotic Fulfillment Program cannot be practiced by everyone.

In much of our research at the Institute for Advanced Psychology, disabled individuals have made a significant contribution to our exploration and understanding of a wide range of extended human capabilities. We therefore request that our disabled readers bear with us, and that they feel free to adapt the various Erotic Fulfillment Program exercises to their personal capabilities and preferences.

We suggest, for example, that if you are blind, hearing impaired, confined to a wheelchair, or otherwise restricted in your ability to easily move around your environment, that you simply adjust the exercises to your particular needs; we assure you that the program will work just as well. We also remind you that many of the Erotic Fulfillment Program exercises are easily adaptable to a wide variety of available sensory and psychological approaches. If necessary, it is completely acceptable to skip a particular exercise, simply replacing it with another more suited to your requirements on a particular day. It is also always acceptable to proceed at a pace that feels most comfortable for you and works best in your individual situation.

We thank you for your interest and participation in the Erotic Fulfillment Program. We hope it will add a new dimension of enriching inner exploration and experience to your life.

Keith Harary and Pamela Weintraub

FOR FURTHER READING

Brauer, Alan P. and Donna J. *The ESO Ecstasy Program: Better, Safer Sexual Intimacy and Extended Orgasmic Response*. New York: Warner Books, 1990.

Chang, Jolan. *The Tao of Love and Sex*. New York: E. P. Dutton, 1977.

Douglas, Nik, and Penny Slinger. *Sexual Secrets: The Alchemy of Ecstasy*. Rochester, Vermont: Destiny Books, 1989.

Lawlor, Robert. *Earth Honoring: The New Male Sexuality*. Rochester, Vermont: Park Street Press, 1989.

Leight, Lynn. *Raising Sexually Healthy Children*. New York: Avon Books, 1990.

McIlvenna, Ted (Ed.). *The Complete Guide to Safe Sex*. San Francisco, CA: Exodus Trust, 1987.

ACKNOWLEDGMENTS

We wish to express our sincere gratitude to our spouses: Darlene Moore, who originated the concept of intuitive sex and inspired many of the exercises in this program; and Mark Teich, who also added to many of the concepts and techniques found within.

We would also like to thank our colleagues and friends who have helped us explore the inner dimensions of human sexuality, especially those whose suggestions and pioneering research we have drawn upon in developing the Erotic Fulfillment Program. Our very special appreciation to the Institute for Advanced Study of Human Sexuality in San Francisco, and especially to Dr. Ted McIlvenna and Dr. Marguerite Rubenstein.

Special thanks also go to our talented and insightful editor, Robert Weil, who came up with the 30-day concept and encouraged us to write this book. We also extend our appreciation to Bill Thomas of St. Martin's Press, for his invaluable insights into the subject matter. Finally, we would like to express our appreciation to our literary agents, Wendy Lipkind and Roslyn Targ.

We also extend our appreciation to the board of directors and board of scientific advisors of the Institute for Advanced Psychology for their role in furthering advanced psychological research.

ABOUT THE AUTHORS

Keith Harary, Ph.D., is internationally known for his pioneering contributions to scientific research on altered states of consciousness and human potential. Dr. Harary, who holds a Ph.D. in psychology with emphases in both clinical counseling and experimental psychology, has authored and coauthored more than sixty popular and professional articles on topics relating to advanced psychological research and other areas. His work has been discussed in dozens of scientific and popular publications and more than two dozen books. He is also coauthor, with Pamela Weintraub, of *Have an Out-of-Body Experience in 30 Days: The Free Flight Program*; *Lucid Dreams in 30 Days: The Creative Sleep Program*; *Mystical Experiences in 30 Days: The Higher Consciousness Program*; and coauthor of the best-selling book, *The Mind Race*. He is President and Research Director of the Institute for Advanced Psychology in San Francisco.

Pamela Weintraub is editor at large at *Omni* magazine, where she has worked on staff for the past nine years. She was previously a staff writer at *Discover* magazine. Her numerous articles have appeared in *Omni, Penthouse, Discover, Health, Ms., Longevity*, and many other national publications. In addition to coauthoring the three books mentioned above with Keith Harary, she is author of *The Omni Book of Interviews*, and *Omni's Catalog of the Bizarre*.

FOR FURTHER INFORMATION ON HUMAN SEXUALITY
RESEARCH AND GRADUATE STUDY OPPORTUNITIES

Institute for Advanced Study of Human Sexuality
1523 Franklin Street
San Francisco, California
94109

(not affiliated with the Institute for Advanced Psychology)

THE 30-DAY HIGHER CONSCIOUSNESS SERIES

Inner Sex in 30 Days is the fourth of an ongoing St. Martin's Press New Age 30-Day series. Also available through your bookstore or by writing to St. Martin's Press are *Mystical Experiences in 30 Days: The Higher Consciousness Program*; *Have an Out-of-Body Experience in 30 Days: The Free Flight Program*; and *Lucid Dreams in 30 Days: The Creative Sleep Program*. All of these titles are written by Keith Harary, Ph.D., and Pamela Weintraub, and can be either specially ordered through your bookstore if currently not in stock, or directly ordered through St. Martin's Press by writing:
St. Martin's Press, Customer Service, 175 Fifth Avenue, New York, New York 10010.
New titles to complement this New Age series will be released in the coming months and subsequent years.
We would like to hear about your experiences with the Erotic Fulfillment Program for possible inclusion in a new book. Please contact us at:

The Institute for Advanced Psychology
Box 875
2269 Chestnut Street
San Francisco, CA 94123